Frontispiece: Nineteenth-century lithograph suggesting pottery's utility, Zulu. From Delessert, *Voyages dans deux Oceans,* 1848. *Courtesy of the Africana Museum, Johannesburg, South Africa.*

ART AND CRAFT OF SOUTHERN AFRICA

Treasures in Transition

RHODA LEVINSOHN

Edited by Barbara LaVine

DELTA BOOKS

DELTA BOOKS (PTY) LTD
A subsidiary of Donker Holdings (Pty) Ltd
P O Box 41021
Craighall
2024

First published 1984

ISBN 0 908387 34 2

Typeset by Triangle Typesetters (Pty) Ltd, Johannesburg
Printed and bound by Colorcraft Ltd, Hong Kong

Contents

All photographs, except where otherwise noted,
by Dr Morris Levinsohn

To my father, Morris Lurie

A believer in tradition
Yet a modern man,
Through his example and his teaching
I have learnt to respect the past
As I anticipate the challenge of the future

Acknowledgements

In expressing my apprectiation to all the people who assisted me in creating this book, which is part of a larger project involving a companion video documentary, I would like to especially thank them for their constant enthusiasm, inspiration, and encouragement. Because of the nature and scope of this work, it was necessary that many different people willingly contribute their talents and knowledge. With me they have shared a genuine interest and desire to document and preserve not only the characteristics of a traditional vanishing culture, but aspects of transition and change, as well.

In showing my gratitude, I would initially like to pay tribute to the talented basket weavers, potters, mural decorators, and bead workers who assisted me in developing a deep understanding and appreciation of their art. They graciously and patiently shared their knowledge and skill with me on many field trips. It was the distinctively adorned women who, especially, broadened my aesthetic awareness and appreciation.

In addition, I am greatly indebted to my faithful interpreters and informants Gaylard Kombani of Gaborone, Botswana; Mr Moshabesha of Maseru, kingdom of Lesotho; Mrs Cecelia Makama and Mrs Dina Mabudafhasi of Johannesburg, South Africa; Mr Tulani Zulu and Mr Ambrose Ngvbese of KwaZulu, South Africa. Reverend and Mrs Kjeil Lofroth of Kwazulu have been invaluable in providing information and assistance, and, over the years, Kingsley Holgate of KwaZulu has shared his tremendous knowledge of Zulu culture with me. Especial thanks are extended to the hereditary Zulu chief, Gatsha Buthelezi, for his encouragement and the inspiration he provided by fostering the art of basketry in his villages. My interview with him was an unforgettable experience.

I am indebted to Dr Barbara Tyrell whose paintings are not only an inspiration, but quite valuable as a source of documentation and reference, while Dr Peter Becker's research and writings have provided a great deal of information. The curatorial staffs of the Africana Museum, Johannesburg; the National Museum, Gaborone; the National Cultural and Open-Air Museum, Pretoria; the Natal Museum, Pietermaritzburg; the Killie Campbell Museum, Durban; and the South African Museum, Cape Town, are to be thanked for giving me access to their ethnographic collections as well as old photographs.

My decision to write this book was finalized when Ms Barbara LaVine, a scholar and erudite young woman, encouraged me to undertake and then spontaneously and enthusiastically agreed to assist me in this mammoth task.

She became totally infused with the people and their culture, grasped a deep understanding of them, and recognized the urgent need to document their endangered vanishing arts and crafts. She not only helped me to clarify my thoughts and synthesize and organize my ideas, but through her editorial judgement and extensive and creative writing, has helped me to produce what I feel is a searching and fascinating manuscript that presents the information and expresses my ideas with a clarity I had not believed possible. It was a pleasure working with Barbara and I extend my sincere gratitude to her.

Heartfelt and sincere appreciation is extended to my husband, Professor Morry Levinsohn, who is responsible, except where otherwise noted, for the excellent photographs taken on numerous field trips to Africa. Through his tool, the lens, he has enabled me and you, the viewer, to see and understand the people and their art more comprehensively. His unfaltering co-operation and encouragement as well as the assistance his shared cultural perspective has brought to this work have been invaluable. His constant enthusiasm and inspiration is a driving force which has enriched my life as well as the lives of those around him, enhancing our appreciation of the culture and decorative arts of the people of southern Africa.

In addition to this book, a colour documentary has been produced by AH Productions, Inc., New York. Because of a genuine concern and a conviction that the cultural past is being shuffled back and will ultimately be forgotten, producer, Anita Lucks, and director, Helen Hyatt, have financed and created a programme to help preserve the precious, fragile crafts of the southern African people. Entitled, 'Art Endangered: A Glimpse of a Dying Craft', it, together with this book, will enable people in every part of the world to view a valuable contribution to art and culture. We may hope that future generations of African artisans will be able to maintain their traditions proudly and retain the basic purpose and appreciation of their history so eloquently captured by this piece. I am ever grateful to AH Productions for their contribution.

For typing the manuscript, my gratitude is extended to Cindy Arenswald whose patience and efficiency are more than appreciated.

Finally, I want to especially acknowledge and thank my children, Karyn and Warren, for keeping house while their mother was on extended field trips to Africa. The enduring patience and understanding they displayed throughout the writing of this book have contributed to the production of a work which, I hope, will assist in fostering an awareness and appreciation of the artistic traditions of the peoples of southern Africa.

Foreword

The appearance of this book attests to a renewed, growing interest in the arts and crafts of what Nelson Graburn and Mrs Levinsohn call the Fourth World. Scholars and patrons have taken it upon themselves to study, acquire and thereby preserve the cultural heritage of societies which by their very nature are marginal, that is, subject to and buffeted by more dominant (although not necessarily superior) cultures and peoples. Autonomy and isolation for most of these peoples are a thing of the past. The Fourth World consists of societies in transition, and since culture is bound up with a people's situation and environment, arts and crafts are changing too, and rapidly. The time frame has been foreshortened. New materials, new techniques, new designs and new functions are introduced virtually before our eyes. It would be a deserving subject in itself to study the agents of these innovations — perhaps applying some version of what geographers have called contagion or alternatively hierarchical theories of diffusion. History moves by fits and starts and presently we are in one of those fitful ages in which, expressed in historical time, in a blink of the eye we may miss a crucial era. Strictly speaking, I suppose, there is no such thing as traditional art. All art is transitional. Some may be more dynamic than others. After centuries of *relative* quiescence, the Fourth World is being exposed to new forces and its cultural expressions are proving to be vulnerable.

Ironically, at the very time that Fourth World arts and crafts are evolving and being replaced, there is a renaissance of interest in traditional art-forms. For some peoples it is a way of recapturing pride and purpose. Jomo Kenyatta's *Facing Mount Kenya* is a Kikuyu nationalist tract as much as it is a serious piece of ethnography. By the same token, entrepreneurs often see such arts in commercial terms, propellants to economic profit and rebirth for the tribe. In regions of economic stagnation, when ambitious men and women leave for greener pastures, efforts to generate local economic activity are vital to the developmental process. Often at the instigation of outsiders who may have a larger perspective on the market for native arts and handicrafts, diverse Fourth World peoples launch modest but frequently successful enterprises.

Their activities represent the apotheosis of 'appropriate technology', costing the community little, and potentially adding a great deal since return on minimal investment can be quite high. These are labour-intensive activities and can be economically sound ventures for a Fourth World people at a

11

'Swallow Formation', *Pelwane Lobopo* motif, Bayei. Gomare village, Ngamiland, Botswana. August 1977.

particular stage of their existence. Carpet making in Iran, pottery for the Pueblo, appliqué for the San Blas Islanders, and knitting in the west of Ireland are just a few examples. Unfortunately for many, the appeal of these activities is limited: 'Tradition wears a snowy beard, romance is always young'. This stage may not last long, but it can be temporarily important, eventually to be replaced by economic pursuits higher up the productive ladder.

At a certain stage there is a danger of becoming commercialized, or at least overly commercial. In its time, it can serve as a way of funnelling money directly into the hands of the primary producers. But twin dangers face these peoples. People may be drawn into the cash economy in which there is a limited market for their output, at least at labour-intensive prices. It also contributes to expectations and demands not easily satisfied by traditional/transitional arts and crafts. It becomes tempting to reorganize the productive process: to move into mass production, as it were. The animal figures carved in Kenya are a case in point. However, authentic forms and designs may become prostituted for the 'tourist trade'. Mrs Levinsohn points up several examples of this in her text. In a way, by succeeding it fails. Quality suffers. Authenticity is compromised. 'Traditional' is maimed. Who cares! The immediate return may be greater as the volume of sales grows. Bad art may make good short-run economic sense. And today's merchants are hardly sticklers for accuracy and authenticity. There is no 'truth in packaging' law for the art market, where *caveat emptor* dances on the casket of historical art-forms.

Students, patrons and *aficionados* of Fourth World arts and crafts soon find themselves on the horns of a dilemma. On the one hand they think of

12

themselves as conservators, protectors and advocates of endangered arts, much like natural conservationists keen on preventing the destruction of a rare species. Yet on the other hand they are accused of trying to freeze dynamic social history, of being paternalistic and patronizing. In so many respects this is a bum rap, for it is possible and quite common for the art lover to be sensitive and aware of this dilemma and yet still allow 'his' people to develop. Is it possible to retain the features of a culture while permitting that culture to evolve? Art is an expression of a people's culture. Can it be divorced from a culture? Of course not. Does that mean that certain art-forms must inevitably be lost as elements of a culture are abandoned? Yes and no. Art collectors can at least preserve good examples of the genre in question. Historians can document and artists and craftsmen can replicate and preserve techniques, designs and forms. But, returning to an earlier point, all cultures change and their arts with them. What we call 'traditional' is only partially so. 'Traditional' Herero dress, the *ohorokueva* so well described in this volume, is a nineteenth-century borrowing from images of Germanic dress. The *basuti* costume in Buganda, likewise, is an adaptation of Victorian modes. Yet we label them 'traditional'. What we are looking for is not static art, but authentic art adapted to the needs and uses of a people. Mrs Levinsohn's book documents this process of arts that are alive, yet endangered almost by their very vitality. This is a universal phenomenon most starkly apparent in southern Africa. It is a subject we must come to appreciate and think about, and Mrs Levinsohn's efforts can start us along that road.

Kenneth W. Grundy, Ph.D.
Professor of Political Science
Case Western Reserve University
Cleveland, Ohio

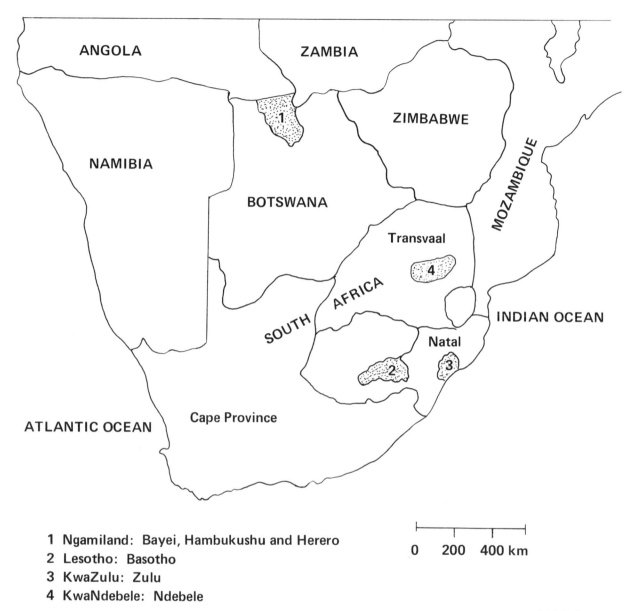

1 Ngamiland: Bayei, Hambukushu and Herero
2 Lesotho: Basotho
3 KwaZulu: Zulu
4 KwaNdebele: Ndebele

MAP 1

Art Endangered

Among the tribal people of southern Africa today there exists a rich and varied centuries-old artistic tradition now endangered by acculturation, the natural outgrowth of the impact of Westernization on these people of the Fourth World. Little known in the West and at the point of an emerging interest in it, a treasure of material arts that expresses the physical and spiritual requirements of indigenous southern Africans is threatened, experiencing a decline so precipitous in the last ten years that urgency must now characterize the need to document what remains before its disappearance is complete.

As Fourth World peoples, the Basotho of the kingdom of Lesotho; the Bayei, Hambukushu, and Herero of Ngamiland, Botswana; the Ndebele of KwaNdebele; and the Zulu of KwaZulu (map 1) are people native to lands falling entirely within the domain of southern Africa. Subject as they are to the demands of the dominant culture, the geographic restrictions within which they have operated have tended, until recently, to protect their culture, traditions, and art from the unavoidable effects of acculturation, the process of becoming adapted to the new cultural patterns that Westernization has wrought on internal cultural expression. Yet, today geographic isolation is insufficient to protect traditional art-forms that are waning and dying out as Western values increasingly replace those of tradition.

The Basotho, Bayei, Hambukushu, Herero, Ndebele and Zulu are by no means the only native southern Africans producing work of note. Their cultures do, however, all share the fundamental criteria upon which this work is based. They all possess traditional arts still functional within their communities, they are all experiencing rapid socio-economic and resulting cultural changes and, finally, as a result of material influences and value shifts stemming from Westernization, they possess living arts that are endangered, that are, in fact, vanishing.

For the past decade, it has become increasingly and alarmingly apparent that these accessible, functional arts that reflect a life-style that is simple yet rich in its ultilization of nature's materials as it reconciles the exigencies of environment, may well disappear into history undocumented, a loss not only to future generations of the people themselves, but to those of us in the West as well. The time is now to document what remains.

Little has been written of the arts of these people. An interest in ethnographic material, expanded to include an overriding concern with the beauty,

ETSHA

OKAVANGO
DELTA

GOMARE

NOKANENG

NAMIBIA

TSAU

SEHITWA

Lake Ngami

BOTSWANA

KALAHARI DESERT

GABORONE

SOUTH AFRICA

MAP 2

16

earthiness, shape, form and design of everyday objects has grown to encompass their architecture, basketry, bead-work, pottery and dress. These art-forms have been selected for consideration because they are icons of their culture depicting the history of a people, their traditions, and cultural milieu. Unlike the commonly recognized African tribal mask, these are relatively little-known arts that provide visual excitement as they stimulate the senses. Their artistic design, aesthetic qualitites, and exoticism warrant more than an ephemeral mention in art history.

One must consider why the graceful art of yesterday and today is the endangered art of tomorrow. Within the complex answer to this most pertinent of questions is to be found clues to the very nature of the art itself. How is it, for example, that internal arts, those objects manufactured, valued, and utilized by the people within their own society, are threatened? These local arts do, after all, play an integral role in preserving cultural heritage, group identity, ethnic cohesiveness and play an educational role as they infuse society's members with traditional values. Yet social conditions exert a profound effect on whether art-forms will survive. Within the context of a rapidly changing social milieu, the lure of the city, new-found occupations, money and the desire for and acquisition of machine-made objects lead to decreased reliance and respect for tradition and the replacement of the hand-made with man- or machine-made articles. Traditional objects produced in a cultural expression, a form of communication linking the past to the present, face a tenuousness that the author, as a romanticist and traditionalist, can only lament.

Unlike the study of an *oeuvre* that represents the artistic expression of a mainstream culture, the arts of the Fourth World require additional contextual grounding in the dominant society within which they exist. Nelson Graburn in his introduction to the text of *Ethnic and Tourist Arts* (1976) raises pertinent questions and points of consideration that form a necessary framework from which the study of an endangered Fourth World art-form should be considered.

The term 'Fourth World', which refers to those native people whose lands are located within the boundaries and political control of countries of the 'first', 'second', and Third worlds, suggests that these are usually minority peoples whose lives are subject to outside control. This is, in fact, the case although the relative degree of autonomy and isolation they once knew has decreased and their arts, like their culture, reflect the exigencies of the dominant culture's influence and tastes.

Graburn's thesis that Fourth World art is the study of changing art accurately describes the state in which indigenous southern African art may be found today. The societies to be considered have all experienced change of one kind or another in a process called acculturation, that was defined by Redfield, Linton and Herskovits as 'those phenomena which result from groups of individuals having differing cultures coming into firsthand contact, with subsequent changes in the original culture of either or both groups.' All societies that interface eventually exchange materials, techniques, and ideas, and this is precisely the situation among the peoples with whom we are concerned here. The work to be studied is testimony to the extent that

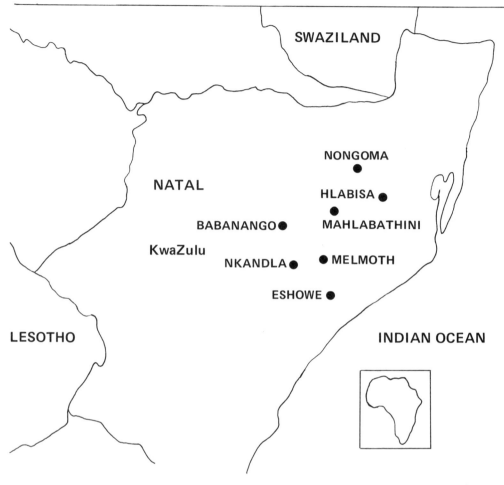

SWAZILAND

NATAL

NONGOMA
●

HLABISA ●

BABANANGO ●

KwaZulu

MAHLABATHINI

NKANDLA ● ● MELMOTH

ESHOWE ●

LESOTHO

INDIAN OCEAN

MAP 3

function need not hinder creativity, artistic beauty, or individualism, at the same time that it provides living, evolving evidence of the demanding effects of extra-societal influences. Even though there is a functional art made primarily for local consumption and, until recently, not intended for external display, outside trade or consumption, it is subject to change and is doing so with a rapidity that reflects the disparity between two societies at different economic and technical levels — a change that is characterized by major alterations in the material culture of the less-developed society. Increasingly, traditional arts and crafts are in direct competition with imported manufactured items and as access to new materials improves, totally new forms develop.

As Graburn suggests:

More important than the availability of new materials and techniques is the advent of new ideas and tastes. Contacts with foreign people, education, literacy, travel, and modern media so broaden the ideas and experiences of Fourth World peoples that they may *want* to change, break away from, or enlarge upon their previously limited traditions.[1]

Graburn notes that the creators of the objects wish to express ideas important to them because

. . . a Fourth World people's 'image' in the eyes of the rest of the world is often as strongly influenced by their portable arts and crafts as by what they actually do in some remote and forgotten homeland or reservation.[2]

He notes that the 'market itself is the most powerful source of formal and aesthetic innovation, often leading to changes in size, simplification, naturalism, grotesqueness, novelty and archaism.'[3]

Market forces have, indeed, affected these art-forms in several ways. As the Western market has developed for these goods, it has reflected the search for the primitive, the handmade, the rare and authentic. At the same time that artists, promoters, and dealers confront the issue of preserving, reproducing or reviving traditional dying arts, in a notable paradox, they must contend with the impetus for change which their very attention has created within the living artistic tradition. The source of the initial attraction in the market-place is thus jeopardized.

While commercial arts intended for outside consumption must satisfy the aesthetic criteria of the foreign buyer and must be viewed as worthy of the collector's attention, those arts intended for internal consumption increasingly reflect the changes stimulated by the market-place as well. At the same time, their extinction, at present a rapidly evolving threat, is the newest dimension of the impact of Westernization and acculturation, and one that has rarely been considered.

The corollary of the paradox previously noted may contain the elements necessary to prevent the extinction of these endangered art-forms as the market-place once again exerts its influence in demanding the creation of an art intended for collectors and museums. As Graburn suggests, the commercial arts (or what he terms pseudo-traditional arts) of these small populations may be made for outsiders only, but they carry the message, 'We exist; we

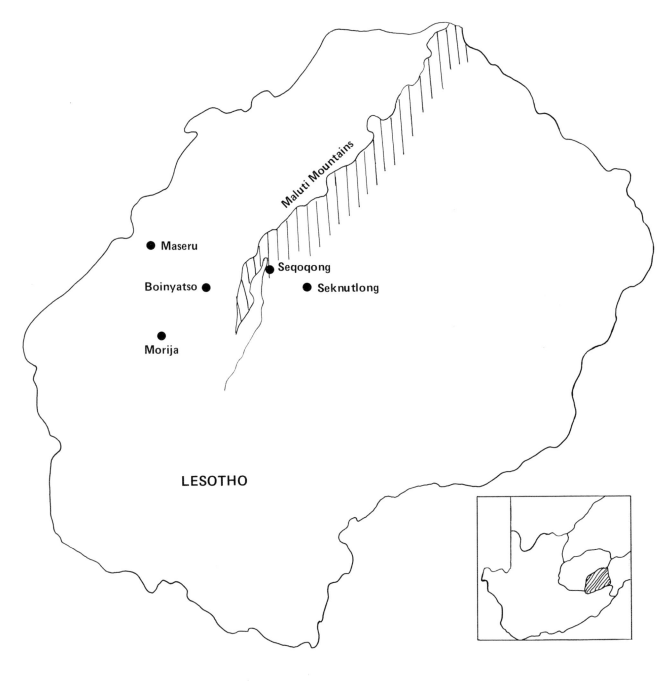

Maseru

Boinyatso

Morija

Maluti Mountains

Seqoqong

Seknutlong

LESOTHO

MAP 4

are different; we can do something we are proud of; we have something that is uniquely ours.'[4] In fact, the essence of the art-form has not yet been lost to Western influences, even as apparent changes have evolved from exposure to Western ideas and a new international marketing system.

Fourth World peoples themselves are also involved in the efforts to preserve, as they often feel the need to highlight and maintain their native customs and values against the pressures from missionaries and the attractions of Western material culture. Although it was the author's experience that the missionaries working independently and those under United Nations auspices played a significant role in preservation, the process is interactive as this same contact leads to the evolution of the artistic forms themselves.

This work is the culmination of study and trips into the field spanning the last decade. The vivid creativity of architecture captured the author's attention initially, although interest in basketry, pottery, Ndebele and Zulu bead-work, Herero dress and dolls soon followed. As the beauty of varied handmade everyday objects was discussed, also noted was the speed with which changes in creative expression were occurring. There arose an urgency to document art-forms endangered by their own beauty and ability to attract the eye of the Westerner, and by the broader effects of Westernization on their creators.

Research included extensive use of materials available in southern African museums. In addition, extensive interviews in the field with the artists themselves were undertaken. This process, of course, provided a wealth of data about the artistic traditions themselves and the socio-cultural evidence attesting to the effects of acculturation. Further, curators of museums and local interpreters and guides offered their perspectives, providing an additional dimension.

Using the architectural unit within which these people live as a base, this work will examine the basketry and pottery used within and outside the homes. The dress worn by the Herero and Ndebele, Herero dolls and Zulu bead-work will, in addition, be examined in a manner that places the art in its socio-cultural context while studying its living evolution.

This is an open-ended art in continuous transition and must be studied as such. By this study, we may learn of the past and present of these fragile Fourth World communities as we confront the tenuousness of their future. We may hope, in a best-case scenario, that dispersion of these art-forms may create a greater interest among existing artisans to continue the art and lure other craftsmen into the production of art-forms that enjoy a marginal existence at present. As Fourth World cultures are at a crossroads so, too, is their artistic expression at a crossroads. It must be hoped that this documentation will not memorialize a dead tradition but bring new life to a rich socio-cultural inconography of the indigenous peoples of southern Africa.

ANGOLA   Diyei   ZAMBIA

Andara

Hambukushu

Bayei

NAMIBIA

0   50 km

BOTSWANA

Gaborone

SOUTH AFRICA

------→ Historical migrations

MAP 5

1 The People:

Their Homes and Habitat

Among the Bantu-speaking tribespeople of southern Africa are the Zulu, Basotho, Bayei, Hambukushu, Herero, and Ndebele. While all are primarily rural people possessing a rich cultural heritage, acculturation is changing the traditions of each at varying but ever-accelerating rates. The material cultures of these people continue, however, to yield valuable evidence attesting to life-style, cultural values, and environmental and artistic traditions at the same time that they increasingly mirror the effects of Western encroachment on their respective life experiences. Their homes, household utensils, clothing and jewellery share the characteristic of possessing a symbolic significance revealing each tribe's notion of beauty, both as the reflection of tribal life-style and effective utlilization of indigenous, readily available materials. While the form this expression takes varies among these people, their dwellings, made by hand like the articles which decorate their homes and adorn their bodies, are an appropriate point of departure from which a study of their material culture may be based.

The traditional sex-determined division of labour marks the construction of homes among the Zulu, Basotho, Bayei, Hambukushu, Herero, and Ndebele. The hewing and arranging of wattle saplings for the framework is the work of the men, while the thatching of grass sheaves and mural decoration is the woman's responsibility. A favourite time for hut building is from June to September before the summer rains, when abundant supplies of thatching grass are available. The grass, collected in the dry season when the seed stalks are fully matured and sun-cured, is bundled, stacked, and made ready for roof building and home improvement. A well-built hut may last five years, although local opinion maintains that if properly cured grass is used, a roof should survive fifteen years. Each tribe described herein employs materials indigenous to their geographic locale and, thus, readily available to them and which, in addition, meet environmental requirements. Whether they be those which meet the exigencies of their traditional techniques of construction or those necessitated by modern modifications, they nonetheless, reflect each tribe's unique assimilation of Western influences. At the same time, their respective histories and traditions of construction are revealed in a distinctiveness of form, setting the dwellings of one tribe apart from those of the others. Those of the Ndebele, for example, possess a uniqueness of design and symbolism that not only warrants but requires separate consideration in a later chapter in this work.

23

The people of the Zulu nation live in KwaZulu or 'Place of Heaven', an area in South Africa between the Transkeian 'homelands' and Swaziland, and within Natal, between the Indian Ocean and the foothills of the Drakensberg escarpment. Among the more well-known of Africans and descendants of several Nguni chiefdoms possessing a distinguished military tradition, they were ultimately united under Shaka, the great nineteenth-century warrior and ruler in the dynasty he created in 1816.[5] For about a fifty-year period thereafter the Zulus first increased the geographic area within their control then suffered increasing military reverses culminating in a period of retrenchment that ended in 1872 with the succession of Cetshwayo, under whom the fine Zulu military machine was once again revitalized.[6]

A new dynamic was now introduced with the white man's intrusion in the form of the High Commission dictate ordering Cetshwayo to demobilize his forces, as well as the subsequent invasion by the British under Lord Chelmsford. Although at Isandlwana the British lost over 600 men in their worst rout since the Crimean War, the outcome saw the defeat and decimation of the Zulu army and Cetshwayo's banishment from the country. At this point, the Zulu nation was subdivided into 13 regions and a period of civil instability followed, carrying with it the seeds of the eventual breakup of the Zulu state and the empowering of white magistrates to administer the areas once controlled by the chieftains.[7] It is because of this period of uninterrupted political instability that radical changes wrought during this time have erased much of the traditional in the lives of the Zulu, making previous history less accessible.

The Zulu possess a kinship tradition characterized by lineages comprising clans, retain a belief in ancestral spirits and initiation schools, and observe a marital ritual that includes the payment of the bride-price. A primarily agricultural people, they live in polygamous homesteads that are similar in form. Their circular, fenced homes include a main hut, a cattle kraal (enclosure), and the huts of the lesser wives located on either side of the great hut. Home to the great wife is the *indlunkulu,* while the *ikhohlwa* is home to the second wife and the *ingqadi* that of the right-hand wife.[8]

Today, among the verdant valleys and undulating hill country of KwaZulu are found these traditional Zulu villages which consist of clusters of grass beehive-shaped huts, *iggugwane,* facing east and the rising sun. (Fig. 1) From the damp valleys, glades, stream banks and swampy areas of this rural area in coastal Natal are available at least forty-five botanical species of reeds, palms, rushes, and grasses not found in other regions of southern Africa. For the hut, the Zulu artisan selects from the variety of plants at her disposal.

To achieve a sound, well-constructed dwelling, a variety of techniques is employed. She begins by arranging sheaves of tall, dry grass in a horizontal position. These sheaves are bundled with a twine, which is made by braiding soft grass according to a technique native to the area, and then stitching together the ends of these long lengths of braid, the same method used to create mats and coiled baskets.

The women then stack bundles of sheaves against the wattle sapling framework of the hut which the men have built, their placement beginning at what

Fig. 1 Typical cluster of huts, Zulu. KwaZulu, South Africa. December 1979.

will later become the small doorway. Once these bundles cover the entire framework, she covers them with large woven grass mats. A network of ropes, *umbige* or *umviko,* made by braiding three bundles of soft grass together, secures the mats to the struts of the framework.[9] This matrix of braided grass, which creates an efficient and ornamental covering, ends in a fully fashioned finial, *inggongwana,* at the top of the hut. (Fig. 2) The result is a dwelling which possesses a natural symmetrical beauty that is distinctly Zulu.

Possessing a background equally as dynamic as that of the Zulu are the Basotho. The Basotho nation, a predominantly Sesotho-speaking agglomeration, was created by the nineteenth-century leader, Moshoeshoe the Great. Inhabiting rural villages or small towns in the kingdom of Lesotho, an independent African state within the Republic of South Africa, they know a feeling of national unity fostered by the legend that all true Basotho originated from the same place, a reed bed at Lake Ntsuanatsatsi, the place where the first man emerged.[10]

While today it is the only country in the world that is entirely 1 000 metres above sea-level, the original Lesotho created by Moshoeshoe included the high plains of the Mohokare (Caledon) Valley, an area lost to modern Lesotho but replaced by the high mountains of the east, the Maluti.[11] Bounded by a series of rivers, the Tele, the Sengu, the Makhaleng, and the Mohokare, the continental divide between the Indian and Atlantic oceans constitutes a portion of the extensive eastern and southern boundaries. While the eastern three-quarters is, to a large extent, inaccessible country, the lowlands of the western quarter are in reality high plains situated 1 500 to 1 600 metres above sea-level and include 7 of the 9 district headquarters' towns, the bulk of the people, and the most fertile land.

25

Fig. 2 Thatched grass beehive hut, Zulu. Kwa-Zulu, South Africa. February 1978.

The typical Lesotho community includes a central home and its surrounding villages. Their rural village existence embodies the observance of traditional customs including chieftancy, belief in ancestral spirits, initiation schools, and marriage ceremonies that include the payment of the bride-price, *bohali*.[12] Unlike the Zulu, the Basotho inhabiting this predominantly rural, mostly mountainous, country have not the variety of grass materials available to them which their hut construction reflects.

Known for their picturesque quality, nonetheless, Basotho villages blend with, enhance, and are enhanced by the hilly, curving, rock-strewn, grey-brown landscape of which they are a part. Encircled by trees and aloes which add to their beauty, the huts are characterized by simple lines, dark brown roofs, and brown and grey walls. The terraced villages rest on sloping hillsides and consist of clusters of circular and rectangular huts built of mud and stone or brick crowned with roofs of thatch. An older type, the *mohlongoafatse,* possessed an oval shape with an elongated entrance built of mud and grass over a framework of sticks, but few of these remain. Facing east for the most part, the dwellings catch the morning sun and avoid the prevailing cold northerly wind.

In Lesotho, when the site of a hut has been chosen, the doorway and mud ledge for household utensils are positioned by the medicine-man with forked twigs made of *mofifi* wood. According to James Walton in his study, *South African Peasant Architecture,* the symbolism of the forked twig is to protect the inhabitants from evil. Another *mofifi* prong placed in the apex of the thatched roof of *mohlomo* grass is said to ward off lightning. The sites of the hut and animal enclosure are sprinkled with magical water to prevent evil and sickness, while small fragments of wood, covered with fat and herbs, are driven into the ground to further protect the inhabitants from misfortune.

26

Fig. 3 *Litema* design on façade of hut, Basotho. Teyateyaneng, kingdom of Lesotho, southern Africa. December 1975.

Thatching of the Basotho huts is usually extremely neat and highly effective against time and the elements. Bundles of *lehlaka* reeds, sewn to the roof framework, act as a foundation before bundles of grass are added. Grass ropes, *thapo,* braided from *moli* grass, comprise the binding for the thatch. Each two-hut household is surrounded by a circular reed screen, the *sectloana.*

Once the hut has been constructed, the women begin the task of decorating the exterior. Motifs may include various patterns of lozenges, circles, zigzags and other geometric shapes which adorn hut walls made of mud, unfired brick, and rubble. (Fig. 3) These materials are bonded with clay and coloured with ocherous pigments.

A design of singular ubiquity is that of the *litema,* one of the most popular which often appears on the cylindrical walls of the rondavels, a circular construction typically 4 metres in diameter, or on the façade of rectangular huts. It consists of parallel grooves arranged in a variety of forms, sometimes suggesting floral patterns. In Basotho symbolism, these grooves represent a ploughed field, *tema.* The women use forks to obtain this striped, furrowed pattern. Using the forefinger, they engrave the walls while the last coat of plastered mud is still wet and, then, with free-hand gestural movements, they imprint the circular design in the wall.

An additional more lasting form of decoration employing a mosaic pattern utilizing embedded stones in mud surfaces is frequently used in the Mafeteng area. Multicoloured stones, usually of brown and white, are selected to form patterns which consist primarily of various combinations of ellipses. (Fig. 4) These mosaic patterns were previously employed in beaded shields used by the Taung people and when they became obsolete, the Taung applied the patterns to their huts as decoration.[13]

27

Fig. 4 Ellipse design of brown and white stone embedded in mud walls, Basotho. Mafeteng, kingdom of Lesotho, southern Africa. December 1975.

In the case of both the Zulu and Basotho and particularly that of the Basotho, villages closest to towns, such as Maseru, are reflecting the impact of modernity. Man-made bricks are replacing the unfired brick or mud walls of tradition, while corrugated iron or tin roofing supplants mud and thatch which is becoming increasingly expensive at the same time that fewer artisans are available to do the actual work of thatching itself. A significant development that imperils this entire tradition is that these new materials are looked upon as desirable since they signify wealth.

Unlike the Zulu and Basotho, the Bayei and Hambukushu are peoples of Zambezi origin who migrated into present-day Ngamiland's Okavango Delta, a swamp and flood plain whose vastness and character delimits the lives of the people it supports. In small and large migrations, both tribes began relocating to the region after 1750. Labelled the Bantu-speaking people from the Middle Zambezi, the Bayei are the largest single entity in Ngamiland and were the first of this linguistic family to reach the Okavango Delta from Diyei or Ngasa, an area now called the Caprivi Strip, located east of the confluence of the Chobe and Zambezi rivers.[14] About the same time, the Hambukushu left Katima Mulilo on the Zambezi River and migrated westward to the Caprivi Strip in Namibia. By the late nineteenth century, they had emigrated further south, settling along the banks of the Okavango River in Namibia and Ngamiland.[15]

While both the Bayei and Hambukushu farmed, raised animals, fished, and hunted, the Hambukushu excelled in cultivation while the Bayei stressed fishing. Their rituals and celebrations reflected these respective strengths although both tribes made offerings to *Nyambi* (God) to maintain productivity.[16] The dislocation of the Hambukushu has continued with their most recent movement, fleeing the wars in southern Angola and Namibia, culmin-

28

ating in their subsequent resettlement at Etsha and Gomare by 1969.[17] Etsha, like the thirteen other villages established at this time, consists of traditional huts (Fig. 5) which house a people who maintain their identity through the retention of the Simbukushu language. Because of the relative isolation of the location, the people settled at Etsha have preserved, to a large extent, many of the traditions of their forebears.

The resettlement of the Bayei and Hambukushu on the Okavango brought the matrilineal cultures of the Zambezi to Ngamiland, and the establishment of a culture based on ultilization of the resources of the flood plain working within the rhythms determined by the flood cycle. Their main source of subsistence is the river from which they fish and gather water roots and other native materials, which they employ in creating the utilitarian articles they require.

Today there are about 40 000 people living in scattered villages around the delta, leading a semi-nomadic existence in that they must continually seek fertile fields and new grazing land for their cattle as dictated by the exigencies of the flood plain. Since residence depends on the season, crops, and plant life which flourish and change with the seasons, there is considerable mobility between their villages and cattle posts, *meraka,* which are not permanent fixtures. Most of the Bayei and Hambukushu tend to require at least two different dwelling places, although even three is not unusual.[18] The abundance of raw materials offered by the Okavango and the geographical isolation of these peoples has, until recently, protected their traditional crafts from competition with commercially produced articles.

While the Bayei and Hambukushu are among the most skilled of all the basket weavers of southern Africa, their architectural construction is less refined. It lacks the artistry of the Zulu and Basotho. (Fig. 6) Reflecting their

29

Fig. 6 Woman winnowing in family compound, Hambukushu. Etsha village, Ngamiland, Botswana, September 1977. *Courtesy of Peter Nelson.*

rather more nomadic life-style, their homes do not feature the concentration on design or detail which lend an aesthetic beauty to Zulu and Basotho villages.

Possessing a simplicity of design, their huts employ palisaded reed walls which enclose extended households. Most dwellings and storage huts are rectangular, with walls of reed mat or wattle, and gabled grass roofs. (Fig. 7) A variety of grasses accumulated in the dry season after the seed stalks have matured and have been sun-cured are employed for thatching. The toughness of the culm cell walls rather than thatch length or thickness is the main requirement, a characteristic determined by the type of grass and the extent to which it has been cured before cutting. In southern Botswana, *Mosasagasolo* grass is the most typical, while the *Mosikiri* variety is gleaned from the sandveld areas near the Kalahari Desert. Taller grasses like *Bojang jarantafulu* are utilized in the north and west, while the *Mosagasolo* is frequently employed in Ngamiland.[19]

The configuration of the dwelling and the village traditionally retains some consistency among the Bayei and Hambukushu. A *utara,* or open shelter, is located to the front of most of the living units. A large cattle kraal is typically located in the centre of the homes, as is the headman's compound, while the gardens for the entire community are within easy walking distance. Increasingly, however, the traditional style of construction has given way to tin-roofed homes of clay brick, which are painted or whitewashed, and growing numbers of people are engaging in brick making, an enterprise whose profitability is burgeoning. This development has led to alterations in the appearance of individual dwellings as well as to changes in the arrangement of the villages themselves.

Sharing the semi-nomadic life-style of the Bayei and Hambukushu are the

30

Fig. 7 Fenced perimeter made of grass, Bayei. Gomare village, Ngamiland, Botswana. August 1977.

Herero, a tribe whose origins are obscure. Over 450 years ago, the Herero, a tall, stately, proud people, began migrating down the west coast of Africa, ultimately settling in regions that include present-day Namibia as well as Ngamiland in northern Botswana. Known commonly as Cattle Damaras, 'People from the West', they comprise four groups: the Herero proper, the Himba, the Tjimba, and the Mbanderu, the principal inhabitants of Botswana today.

Possessing a cultural tradition based on cattle herding, they have not engaged in agricultural pursuits, depending on cattle for their diet with occasional supplements of wild vegetables. In the 1800s, the wealth of their cattle holdings drew the attention of German colonialists who increasingly attempted to seize their rather substantial herds. As a result of their subsequent revolt, the culmination of years of increased German encroachment on their herds, the Herero lost all of their cattle and were forced to consolidate their settlements in northern Botswana.

Prospering rapidly, however, they rebuilt their herds and achieved an economic independence by 1934 that subsequently led to their present position as the mainstay of Botswana's cattle industry. This development represents a major evolution in Herero culture since cattle were formerly held sacred and an individual's wealth was measured by the size of his herd. Now that the Herero actively market their cattle, they have lost their traditional religious organization and with it, ancestor worship. As a result, one's descent no longer detemines role or regulates behaviour as in the past.[20] These changes have evolved over seventy years having begun when the Herero arrived in Botswana following their defeat at the Battle of Waterberg in August 1904. Cattle are now viewed as a market commodity rather than centrepieces of cultural ritual, and this development has affected all facets of their culture,

31

Fig. 8 Clay-walled and thatched-roofed rondavel, Herero. Maun, Ngamiland, Botswana. August 1977.

bringing changes to every aspect of their life-style.

Like the Bayei and Hambukushu, the Herero live in villages, *werfs*, which face east and are constructed according to a relatively consistent circular plan. Housing a community of relatives since intermingling of diverse families is forbidden by custom, the village is composed of homesteads consisting of one or more household clusters, the largest residential unit.[21] Because Herero men are often polygamous, the wives usually construct separate household clusters. Frequently, often due to this situation, homestead or household residents work together in ritual, economic, and political activities. Household residents label their group an *onjuo*, 'those of the house', and invoke their mothers' names to label their settlement.[22]

The Herero huts are of the rondavel style, a round, beehive shape. (Fig. 8) Their framework is of stout branches, the lower ends of which are forced into the earth, while the uppermost ends are gathered together and fixed with bark. To support a rondavel thatched roof, heavy posts of the Mopane tree are required although, when these are unavailable, Mokoba poles are used. These vertical supports are called *maotwana* and it is to these that a varied number of poles are fixed to create the roof's framework. Coming together at the peak, they are tied to one another and to a cross segment fastened to at least two or three poles. These perpendicular roof poles, *ditlhomeso*, are similar to rafters and are normally made of Mopane, although Mokoba or Mogonoma are sometimes employed.[23] To this framework is added a covering of brushwood or long grass which is coated with a mixture of cow dung and clay. In the rainy season, the huts receive an additional covering of raw hides secured by large stones. The hut's entrance is composed of a hole through which a person may gain entrance by creeping on all fours. Today, wooden doors are used. Cow dung coats the floor although skins are spread upon it to serve as beds.[24]

The semi-nomadic condition in which the Herero live explains the simplicity of construction and design of their dwellings, but it is the effects of acculturation that, once again, are causing alterations in their architecture. At the same time that the assimilation of Western values has stimulated the people's inclination to build with modern materials like concrete and corrugated iron, it has been noted that oftentimes this decision has stemmed from a paucity of traditional materials. The fact is that materials of either sort have risen in price in recent years to make housing a financial problem for increasing numbers of people.

Nonetheless, traditional roofing has increased recently for a variety of reasons, some economic, some social, and others aesthetic. A renewed interest in ensuring the charm and architectural distinctiveness of the traditional in tandem with the inflated costs of the imported materials is tending to mitigate the trend towards modern building techniques. Furthermore, climatic conditions often favour thatched edifices which are more appropriate for cool summers and warm winters in locales like Botswana, for example. In addition, traditional construction is more conducive to separate living units typical of most family courtyards in which different sexes and generations possess separate rondavels, while grain storage and cooking are limited to additional rondavels. Not only do separate living quarters with their enhanced ventilation reduce the risks of infectious diseases, but those of fire damage, as well.

We have seen that the dwellings of the Zulu, Basotho, Bayei, Hambukushu and Herero, mirror the impact of environment and history on these people. At the same time that these factors frequently work similar limitations to a tribe's aesthetic expression, however, they may also preclude a sameness in character, a condition readily discerned from observation. In any case, at present, several dynamics are working on the architectural characteristics of their tribal homes, and both stem directly or indirectly from the influences of Westernization.

Cultural value change, modern materials of construction, and inflation are dimensions that hold the key to the currently threatened survival of the traditional. In the end, however, it may be the most Western of dynamics, inflation, that is the factor upon which the outcome will turn. In competition with an urge to modernize is the fact that traditional building materials are, in some cases, increasingly less expensive than the new. In addition, as economic retrenchment reduces opportunity and diminishes incentive, the people, the young especially, may rediscover the beauty and value of indigenous forms. The trend is leaning towards modernization, however, and 'tenuous' must describe the current position of traditional architecture in southern Africa.

Following page: Fig. 18 Typical basket used for carrying, *iqoma*, Zulu. Hlabisa village, KwaZulu, South Africa. January 1980. *Courtesy of Peter Nelson.*

33

2 Basketry:

Reflection of a Tradition

Basket making among the tribal people of southern Africa is a long-established art in transition. Fulfilling as it does the utilitarian requirements of everyday and ceremonial tribal life, it is numbered amid the most firmly rooted of historical traditions among the Zulu, Bayei, Hambukushu, and Basotho, the ethnic entities within the scope of consideration here. An art typically handed down from one generation to the next by the women, there is a standard of form and technique distinctive to each tribe, while inter-tribally, variations of design as well as construction distinguish the work of one tribe from that of another. Yet, as acculturation's impact has affected each tribe's life-style according to individual characteristics of geographical location, habitat, and ecology, the basketry tradition of each has been marked by a diversity of response ranging from rejuvenation of a dying tradition to virtual extinction of this decorative art. Especially attractive to the Western eye and a form with which the collector may readily identify, the marketability of this easily transported art-form has, for the present, ensured the continuation of a faltering art-form at the same time that this extraterritorial dissemination is threatening the very existence of the art-form itself. Thus, this highly commercial indigenous African art is evolving at a speed and in a manner that increasingly reflects the demand nature of the market-place, while its unique attraction carries with it the potential disappearance of this most functional and integral of African tribal artistic traditions.

The earliest available evidence reveals that, at least as far back as 1849, basketry fulfilled the functional and ceremonial requirements of daily life among the tribal peoples of southern Africa, while circumstantial evidence suggests that their use antedates this era. Old lithographs indicate that royalty and community members alike made use of baskets of diverse form. (Fig. 9) From 1880 on, more documentation exists attesting to the central role baskets held in these cultures, (Fig. 10) a development which can be attributed to the new interest in the natural resources of southern Africa born of the discovery of gold and diamonds. The exploitation of these resources brought with it the growth of towns and industry and the establishment of museums. The curiosity of indigenous Africans and Europeans alike was aroused about the native people and their life-styles. It was at this time that the renowned Dr David Livingstone lived among the people, and it is his illustrations, as well as those of G.F. Angas, that depict the character of basketry in this era. (Fig. 11)

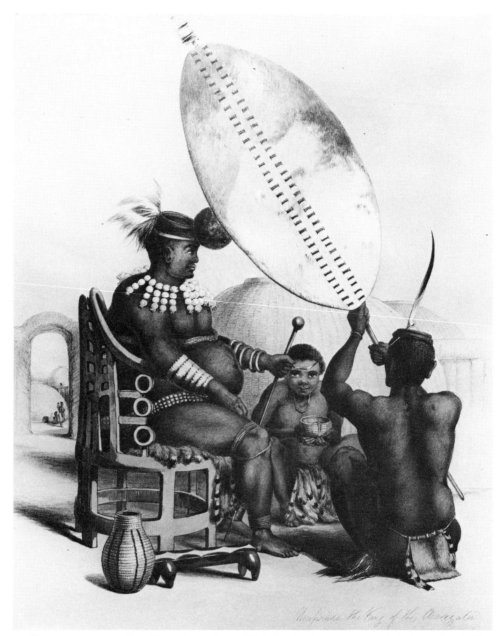

Fig. 9 Lithograph depicting basketry as employed by royalty, Zulu. Drawn by the artist G.F. Angas, 1849. *Courtesy of the Africana Museum, Johannesburg, South Africa.*

36

Then, as now, the functions to which basketry were put determined the characteristics of the baskets individual tribes fashioned. There were, as there are today, a number of basic shapes of woven articles constructed to fulfil utilitarian domestic needs. These traditional items, (Fig. 12) which may show some variation in size or construction, include bulb-shaped baskets, lidded pot-shaped containers, flask-shaped baskets, and flared or saucer-shaped bowls. Collectively, the people use baskets for storage of liquids or dry foods, agricultural activities, and transportation of food or fuel. Each of these functions require baskets of different shapes and construction.

Fig. 10 Engraving illustrating the role of baskets in daily life, *iqoma*, Zulu. From D. Livingstone, *Missionary Travels and Researches in Southern Africa*, 1880. *Courtesy of the Africana Museum, Johannesburg, South Africa.*

    Bulb-shaped baskets are typical of the woven containers that are still used for storing liquids. (Fig. 13) This type of container plays a major role in the preparation and serving of beer, a beverage of central importance in the African culture. Beer is not merely a thirst-quenching beverage, but rather a major part of many social traditions. Sorghum-derived beer, regarded as a staple, is drunk daily, as well as at all ritual and ceremonial festivals, including weddings, before a funeral, and at the end of an agricultural work party.

Fig. 19 Typical basket used for carrying, *setego*, Bayei. Gomare village, Ngamiland, Botswana. August 1977.

38

Fig. 20 Typical basket used for carrying, *thikote*, Hambukushu. Etsha village, Ngamiland, Botswana. August 1977.

39

Fig. 11 Wood engraving depicting utensils, nineteenth century, Zulu. L. Shooter, *The Kaffirs from Natal*, 1887. *Courtesy of the Africana Museum, Johannesburg, South Africa.*

40

In a society in which the family or clan predominates over the individual, beer is the drink that is served to bind groups of people together. In these cultures, the serving of beer is a symbol of hospitality, the most important social occasion being the feast which brings with it the promise of food and, above all, the consumption of beer.[25] For these people who maintain a strong belief in ancestral spirits, diviners, and herbalists, beer often serves as a votive offering to ancestral spirits. As Barbara Tyrell, an expert on Zulu folkways, has written:

Fig. 12 Wood engraving depicting utensils, nineteenth century, Zulu. L. Shooter, *The Kaffirs from Natal,* 1887. *Courtesy of the Africana Museum, Johannesburg, South Africa.*

Important ritual attaches to the serving of traditional beer. It must be presented and received in a respectful attitude, either squatting, kneeling, or seated. It is stored (in the bulb-shaped basket) in the hut in a special place where the spirits of the ancestors dwell, opposite the door.[26]

These social and ritualistic connotations of beer drinking endow the woven artefacts used in the preparation and serving of beer with special significance.

The Zulu *isichumo* (Fig. 14) and the Bayei *serotwana* (Fig. 15) are examples of large bulb-shaped baskets made of palm leaf which are used for carrying, storing, and serving beer. These containers are tightly woven and when beer or liquid is poured into them, the inner follicles swell, making the vessels watertight. Some Zulu *isichumo* are spherical with a cylindrical neck, 7,5 to 10 centimetres in height, while others have a flared neck featuring a lid or cap. The lip of the *isichumo* is usually finished off with a fine herringbone stitch, and dyed ilala filaments add decoration to the natural background. For the construction of these baskets, the coiled or figure-eight weaving technique is employed.

Pot-shaped containers are made by the Zulu and Bayei to store and carry liquids, as well. The Zulu pot-shaped basket, the *ukhamba,* (Fig. 16) designates both an earthenware pot and a particular kind of basket. Smaller than the bulb-shaped basket, it is cylindrical featuring a wide mouth, and may be plain or embellished. These pot-shaped baskets share a relationship with coiled pottery in form and function. Like those of the Zulu, the Bayei pot-shaped basket, the *serotwana,* is smaller than the bulb-shaped constructions. Usually cylindrical, they feature a broad girth and possess a wide mouth which facilitates their use. Baskets 30 centimetres in diameter and 30 centi-

41

Fig. 21 Typical basket used for carrying, *seroto*, Basotho. Seqoqong village, kingdom of Lesotho, southern Africa. August 1977.

Opposite page: above, Fig. 28 Affinity of jewellery and basketry design displayed, Zulu. *Author's collection, 1982; below,* Fig. 29 Triangular, zigzag and diamond motifs adorn lidded baskets, Zulu. *Author's collection, 1982; following page,* Fig. 13 Watertight beer storage basket, *serotwana,* Bayei. Gomare village, Ngamiland, Botswana. August 1977.

42

Fig. 14 Woman construct-
ing bulb-shaped beer bas-
ket, *isichumo,* Zulu. Melmoth, KwaZulu, South
Africa. January 1980.
Courtesy of Peter Nelson.

metres in height are typical. The Hambukushu, on the other hand, create
lidded, flask-shaped baskets to store and carry liquids. (Fig. 17)

The flared bowl, constructed to meet the diverse functions of the agricultural activities of rural people, varies in width, depth, size and design.
Because of its adaptability, the traditional flared bowl is, in fact, the basket
which is most commonly found in rural areas. Saucer-shaped, larger versions
of these flared, woven baskets are used by the women for winnowing, that
is, for allowing the wind to blow away the chaff and impurities of their grain.
Sometimes, two baskets are used in this process, so that, in addition to
throwing the grain into the air, one can pour it from one basket to another.
In addition, the flared bowl is used as a flour container, a typical example of
which is the Bayei *setego* with its flat, circular, base-slanted sides. The Zulu
iqoma (Fig. 18), the Bayei *setego* (Fig. 19), the Hambukushu *thikote* (Fig.
20), and the Basotho *seroto* (Fig. 21) are those baskets women use to
balance on their heads when grain, fruits, vegetables or cow dung must be

Following page: above, Fig.
30 Bold geometric pat-
terns predominate on typically symmetrical baskets,
Zulu. *Author's collection,
1982; below,* Fig. 31 One
weaver's use of triangular
designs, Zulu. *Author's
collection, 1982.*

45

Fig. 32 Elina Mhlongo completes a pot-shaped basket of popular zigzagged multicoloured design, Zulu. Hlabisa village, Kwa-Zulu, South Africa. August 1979.

47

48

carried a long distance. Accordingly, the diameter of these baskets is often about the width of the wearer's shoulders, while the base is small and sometimes slightly domed to facilitate balance.

Although the weaver's art is largely based on manual dexterity, the weavers supplement their skill with tools both found and purchased. Of the cutting tools, the largest is the axe, purchased and used for hacking coarse material like branches, bark, or roots, while sickles are employed to cut long sheaves of grass. A large knife is used for cutting less coarse material, while penknives or short, sharp knives. which fit snugly in the palm, are used for preparing and scraping raw material. Blades for splitting leaves, as well as trimming edges, are also utilized. Metal containers such as buckets, pails, bowls, or discarded clay pots are employed for soaking materials in water and for moistening the worker's hands. The pots keep the water and raw material cool while the traditional African wrought-iron tripod pot, *pitsa,* acts as a mordant when the leaves are boiled in vegetable dyes prepared from indigenous roots, bark, bushes, leaves, rusty chains, or metal cans. The leaves are left to soak in the *pitsa* pot into which the weavers also dip their hands, wetting them to facilitate the weaving process. Before the weaver begins, he or she ensures that the necessary tools are at hand: a bowl of water, a knife, split leaves, a pounding stone, and an awl. (Fig. 22)

Fig. 17 Flask-shaped baskets featuring distinctive overstitch, Hambukushu. Etsha village, Ngamiland, Botswana. February 1982.

The weavers refer to the beginning of the basket as the 'embryo' (Fig. 23) and, once begun, its growth progresses as a tenuous strand as the foetus is bound firmly and evenly around the foundation or 'mother'. (Fig. 24) Figure-eight coiling continues until the basket has reached the necessary shape and size desired by the weaver. (Fig. 25) If the coils are tightly woven, the baskets will not only be watertight, but also have great strength and durability. (Fig. 26)

Although the Zulu, Bayei, Hambukushu, and Basotho produce similar baskets, different characteristics, primarily those of design, distinguish the work of one tribe from that of another. Simply stated, Zulu work features symmetrical overall design, while the Bayei and Hambukushu produce both symmetrical and asymmetrical designs with those of the Hambukushu often featuring an overstitch treatment not to be found in the work of the other tribes. The work of the Basotho is marked by a complete absence of design.

Zulu craftsmen favour symmetry, precision, and organization in the designs of their basketry – qualities which seem to distinguish their social patterns. The traditional arrangement of their village is in the form of a circle, which represents the woman as a symbol of birth, while the huts that constitute the village symbolize the seeds from which it develops. This organization is reflected in their crafts and basketry, in particular.

Typically covering the entire surface of the basket, the Zulu's symmetrical designs share a close affinity to those of their bead-work. The Zulu create beaded body jewellery because they place great emphasis upon the adornment of their women. As a Zulu child grows up, for example, the types of beads worn indicate the transition from one developmental stage to another, as they symbolize rank, courtship, and marriage rituals. As such, Zuly bead-work is an integral part of their cultural tradition. (Fig. 27) It is no surprise

Fig. 22 Weaver shown with tools and materials required for basket making, Hambukushu. Etsha village, Ngamiland, Botswana. August 1977.

that these designs have infected their basketry as well.

The designs found on some Zulu baskets, then, are visually similar to those found on their bead-work, possessing a sense of proportion created by heavy overall patterning. (Fig. 28) The use of triangles, zigzags, diamond shapes and rectangular motifs predominates, utilizing weaving technique and colour to enhance their execution. (Fig. 29) Many weavers interviewed said that they were inspired by the traditional bead-work and that this source of inspiration had influenced the decorative designs on their basketry. This influence is revealed in a number of examples where bold geometric patterns predominate. (Fig. 30) In these baskets, the entire surface has been embellished with elaborate diamond, triangle, or rectangular designs. (Fig. 31) These compositions are aggregations of simple forms which are the alphabet of the Zulu woman's most intricate patterns. Stylistically, the surfaces do not remain inert, but aesthetically unified and elaborate.

As recently as 1979, a new characteristic had been observed in Zulu basketry, the introduction of heretofore unavailable colours. Obtained by boiling the bark of the *umkanu* and *umquenju* trees, and the leaves of the *nphekambendu* bush for five to seven hours, mauves and pinks of varying hues have been captured. Incorporating these hues with the traditional orange from the *umdoni* tree and dark brown dyes from the *isinsimane* tree root, a number of weavers including Tsolslosla Msaolgo, Elizabeth Masuka, Elina Mhlongo (Fig. 32), Florence Mhlonga, Sizakele Hlabisa, and Flora Hlabisa, all of Hlabisa village, are successfully incorporating this new colour into their designs. The combination of subtle colourations with facile execution of design have increasingly distinguished Zulu work, setting it apart from that of the Hambukushu and Bayei to whom we now turn.

Well north of Johannesburg, in the northernmost part of Botswana in

51

Fig. 23   A basket's beginning, embryo, Hambukushu. Etsha village, Ngamiland, Botswana. September 1979. *Courtesy of Peter Nelson.*

Ngamiland, are the Hambukushu and Bayei, the largest of the basket-weaving tribes in this area. The Bayei are skilful in the ultilization of their environment which has led to a vibrant and prolific basket-making tradition among them. Masters of the river, its delta, and the surrounding flood plain, they use the indigenous reeds and other flora of the river and surrounding swamps to make those items required for everyday use. The Hambukushu arrived in this region in the late nineteenth century and settled along the banks of the Okavango River, bringing with them their cultural traditions, knowledge of the swampy environment, and their weaving technique.

Their work shares many similarities with that of the Bayei. Both produce designs featuring large, geometric patterns which are predominantly asymmetrical. Any one basket may possess a variation of design stemming from the combination of motifs and their asymmetrical arrangement. This irregularity may reflect their social structure and habits. Mobile people, both tend to have two or three different dwelling places, one in their village and others at the cattle posts, *meraka,* where the people live temporarily while herding their cattle to the grazing grounds.[27] In addition, they are often forced to move because of droughts, floods, and infestations of the tsetse fly.[28] It is arguable that this life-style fosters a greater freedom and flexibility in their art, since their baskets, for example, show a diversity of design uncommon to the work of the other tribes. Their freedom of movement may create the mind-set that permits the flexibility of motif and asymmetry that marks their basketry. (Fig. 33)

Especially typical of Hambukushu weaving is an embroidery overstitch of like or dissimilar colour that is added to the basket in the process of coiling. Designs achieved through this stitch variation can be seen in a number of Hambukushu bowls in which the embroidery stitch added to the basic coiled

52

Fig. 24 Basket grows as a filament (mother), wraps the fibre bundle (child), Zulu. Hlabisa village, Kwa-Zulu, South Africa. September 1980. *Courtesy of Peter Nelson.*

Following page: Fig. 25 Completed coiled basket, *isichumo*, Zulu. Hlabisa village, KwaZulu, South Africa. August 1977.

53

Fig. 26 Unusually large storage basket, *serotwana*, Bayei. Gomare village, Ngamiland, Botswana. January 1980. *Courtesy of Peter Nelson.*

Fig. 27 Geometric jewell-
ery design which inspires
basketry design, Zulu.
*Courtesy of the Africana
Museum, Johannesburg,
South Africa.*

stitch flares outward in a complex series of petal-like shapes. (Fig. 34) Here
the overlapping stitches control the pattern which appears on both the interior
and exterior. Not only is the texture of visual interest, but the decorative
stitching serves a functional purpose; it prevents the finely ground flour that
the women pour into the baskets from adhering to the walls.

At the same time, however, a small number of Hambukushu and Bayei
weavers create symmetrical designs. Dyed fronds are often used to vary design, the effects ranging from subtle colourations to intricate patterns featuring a variation of motifs. The use of triangles, zigzags, diamond and rectangular shapes, and chequer-board figures can be used separately or in combination. Designs often reflect the influence of bead-work designs as the weavers,
like the Zulu, report inspiration from traditional bead-work, a ceremonial
reflection of their culture. While black and white are used to create contrast
in their bead-work, their basketry designs echo this patterning, although in
more muted colours. In the basketry pieces, the natural coloured fronds
parallel the bead-work's white background, while the brown designs used as
an accent colour when woven into the containers, parallel the black of the
bead-work. (Fig. 35) Patterns of dramatic simplicity result from the rhyth-
mic effect obtained by zigzag forms and triangular shapes used vertically and
horizontally. In some instances, a striking arrangement of positive-negative
imagery creates an integrated combination of motifs. (Fig. 36) Whatever
their origins, both the Bayei and Hambukushu incorporate geometric and
imaginary designs in their work. However, that which is particularly unique
to the baskets of the Bayei is their use of symbolic design.

56

Fig. 33 Typical symmetrical motifs, Bayei. Gomare village, Ngamiland, Botswana. July 1982.

Fig. 34 Petal-shaped motifs woven with typical embroidered overstitch, Hambukushu. Etsha village, Ngamiland, Botswana. July 1982.

The Bayei, unlike the Hambukushu, Basotho, and Zulu weavers, have evolved a series of symbolic patterns which are not confined to specific families but are shared within the Bayei community. These patterns are called by specific names by the weavers. These names all relate to nature, especially to the animals that live in the desert. According to Gaylard Kombani, a local co-ordinator for the propagation of the basketry of that region,

Traditionally, most of the designs resemble patterning found on animal skins, or relate to some aspect of animal life. After a hunt, the weavers would keep records of what animals looked like. They chose a certain part of the killed animal and then evolved its design into basketry.[29]

The Bayei's constant contact with nature and perception of animal life pro-

57

Fig. 35 Bead-work and basketry designs mirror one another, Bayei. Gomare village, Ngamiland, Botswana. August 1977.

vided the stimulus to imitate and express those observations in an art-form.

Perhaps the most striking design among the Bayei is the 'Forehead of the Zebra' (*Phatla ya Pitsa*). The careful observation of the zebra with its characteristic pattern of black stripes on a whitish background has been effectively portrayed in several pieces. (Fig. 37) The use of heavy and thin zigzag lines, creating a pattern of movement, fills the entire space of the containers. Each artisan, by infusing her own ideas and imagination into the basic design, alters the pattern to some degree.

Another popular design of the region is the 'Tail of the Swallow' (*Sentiia ya Pelwana*). The darkly curved triangular motif resembling the deeply forked tail of the swallow is arranged in a circular pattern in the inner section of the basket. The same motif is repeated as an ornamental border. (Fig. 38) The addition of curved lines in some of the baskets gives an illusion of movement, like the graceful, swift flight of the swallow. One craftsperson, Kejemg Matengwe, states that she learned the Tail of the Swallow design from her grandmother.[30] Her representation of the two large 'tails' includes a diamond motif, the shape of which she recently saw on playing cards. (Fig. 39) The striking aspect of this basket is the combination of an old motif (from grandmother) and the addition of a new motif (diamond from cards). Further variations on the 'swallow' theme are found in other baskets, where groups of triangles are connected to form one large triangle and are thus said to depict a 'Swallow Formation' (*Pelwane Lobopo*).

Another distinct design woven by the Bayei is the 'Knees of the Tortoise' (*Manole a Khudu*), in which bold angular lines point towards the centres of the baskets. (Fig. 40) The acute and obtuse angles of the 'knees' represent joints that permit movement. As Gaylard Kombani observes:

Fig. 36 Positive-negative imagery marks flared bowls and bulb-shaped baskets, Bayei. Gomare village, Ngamiland, Botswana. July 1982.

The tortoise is a very useful animal to Botswana's desert dwellers. Roast tortoise is considered a great delicacy, especially its delicious liver. The shell is plunged into boiling water for a few minutes, then the meat is pulled out and roasted in the ashes. The shell is retained so that it can be made into a medicine bag and used as a utensil by witch-doctors and Bushmen.[31]

An unusual example of these Knees-of-the-Tortoise baskets is one in which the weaver has reversed the colours, thus creating an arrangement of a positive-negative combination. (Front left of Fig. 40)

An additional design symbolizing an aspect of animal life is the 'Tears of the Giraffe' (*Dikelede ya Thutlwa*). 'Long ago the hunters would chase and shoot giraffes. The giraffe cries before he dies and leaves a trail of tears', weaver Dikgang Rasekete explains.[32] The jagged lines of a typical representation represent the spilt tears of the giraffe. While working on the broken lines to represent the flowing 'tears', Bayei weaver Khiana Xania indicated that she had acquired this design from her mother. She adheres to the traditional designs but also adds imaginative decoration, such as triangular and rectangular shapes spaced at irregular intervals.

One of the simplest designs woven by the Bayei weavers is referred to as 'Urine of the Bull' (*Moroto wa Makaba*). Here, irregular, wandering lines follow the contour of the basket in an upward direction to depict the imprinted trail of the spilt fluid as it is left on the dry desert.

Symbols relating to history have provided still another source of inspiration for the basket weavers. A striking example of a historical symbol ex-

Fig. 37 'Forehead of the Zebra' (*Phatla ya Pitsa*) design, Bayei. Gomare village, Ngamiland, Botswana. *Author's collection, July 1982.*

Fig. 38 'Tail of the Swallow' (*Sentiia ya Pelwana*) design, Bayei. Gomare village, Ngamiland, Botswana. August 1977.

pressed in the fibre arts is the 'Shield' (*Thebe*) design, the shield symbolizing protection and strength. Shields of untanned cowhides were used as a means of protection against opposing tribes and wild animals. The placement of darkened triangles in emphatic vertical formation, dominating the design and contrasting with thin lines, represents an arrangement of shields, perhaps akin to that which one would see if observing a regiment of warriors.

Conventionalized representations of animal forms as a whole are depicted

60

Fig. 39 Kejemg Matengwe
completes 'Tail of the
Swallow' design, Bayei.
Gomare village, Ngami-
land, Botswana. August
1977.

61

Fig. 40 'Knees of the Tortoise' (*Manole a Khudu*) design, Bayei. Gomare village, Ngamiland, Botswana. August 1977.

only by the Hambukushu weavers. Typical examples are simplified renditions of deer. Other animal design elements, such as the donkey, a domestic animal used by the villagers for pack carrying and transportation, ostriches, and dogs, as well as figurative motifs, are used repeatedly by the Hambukushu weavers. (Fig. 41)

In many baskets, the design is complex in the sense that the weavers use a combination of motifs. There are symbolic representations of the elements, birds and animals, subject-matter important to people who live close to nature. The complexity of design is intentional, not merely imitative, and the symbols woven in juxtaposition bear significance in the mind of the weaver. In looking at the use of traditional designs, the weavers seem to have a desire to perpetuate familiar designs taught to them. This preference for perpetuating their heritage from one generation to another may reflect their desire for continuity with the past, their interest in animals and the elements, or it may reflect their confinement to rural life.

As suggested earlier, acculturation has affected the basket weavers of southern Africa in diverse ways, and in the case of the Basotho, Westernization's effects have threatened their craft to the extent that this material tradition is all but extinct. Several factors have led to the demise of this art-form among these people of Lesotho, however, not the least of which is the nature of the baskets themselves. The Basotho neither decorate their pottery, nor adorn their bodies with beaded ornament. Lacking an interest in this form of design, it is not surprising, then, that their baskets remain simple utilitarian implements lacking embellishment. Their simplicity, therefore, has had less appeal in the market-place as tourists and collectors have confined their attention to the decorated Zulu, Bayei, and Hambukushu baskets.

Fig. 41 Unique animal motifs worked into asymmetrical compositions, Hambukushu. Etsha village, Ngamiland, Botswana. *Author's collection, July 1982.*

The basket-making tradition that is struggling to survive among the Basotho is one that was handed down from one generation to the next and was practised by both the men and the women. (Fig. 42) Their country is a mountainous one, consisting, in small part, of grasslands which are under the sole control of the chief, who, on behalf of the king, informs the people of the location for grass collecting when the time is right, in the spring.

The collection of grasses accomplished, the Basotho men and women prepare metres of braided grass roping. To make these braided filaments, the artisan takes bundles of soft grass and, in a seated position, clutches the bundles between the toes. By continuing this braiding process, the weaver produces long lengths of rope which are coiled to fashion the *seroto,* their flared bowl. (Fig. 43) This most common of Basotho baskets, constructed almost entirely of twine, sometimes possesses a horsehair-trimmed rim for firmness and strength, along with a circular hide pad to reinforce the base. It is customary among them that when the women commence winnowing, they face northeast towards Lake Ntsuanatsatsi 'as it was there we used to live'.[33] When they lift up their second basketful, they face their own hut. The basket is never emptied, retaining a few grains to be tossed on to a heap of unwinnowed grain before the women scoop up another basketload. It is their belief that this custom will preserve the continuity of the agricultural cycle.[34]

While the precipitous decline in Basotho basket making stems from the inability to compete with the more decorative versions of the Zulu, Bayei and Hambukushu, their dwindling manufacture is due, in large part, to cultural changes. Claiming a ninety-seven per cent literacy rate, the Basotho include increasing numbers of people who are seeking employment away from the villages, and this development has engendered in them the desire to modernize, to appropriate articles of Western manufacture for their convenience and status. Sacking and large drums are rapidly replacing the traditional woven items, chicken-wire is supplanting the traditional beer strainer, and the

63

Fig. 42 A pencil sketch drawn by artist Hermon, 1895, Basotho. *Courtesy of the Africana Museum, Johannesburg, South Africa.*

demand for baskets is relatively small outside the villages. Although a native Basotho, Malefane Malefane, actively buys and promotes local handicrafts, and Dr Biemans, director of Lesotho Handicrafts, encourages and promotes basket making out of a strong sense of concern that this fragile tradition be continued, the decline in basket production among the Basotho continues.

While the basket-making tradition among the Basotho is most endangered by the impact of Westernization, those of the Zulu, Bayei, and Hambukushu are in the midst of a revival, albeit one that reflects the direct impact of Western taste and deliberate effort to preserve this rich artistic tradition. The past decade has seen both a renewed interest in basket making among the tribal people themselves, and the growth of a hitherto nonexistent recognition and appreciation of the art-form among outsiders. Instigated through the efforts of handicraft developers, missionaries, government agencies, and other patrons, an interest in preserving and nurturing this age-old art-form has evolved. The craft as it obtains today, however, is in transition since acculturation has increasingly altered tribal life-styles and values at the same time that Western market forces place new aesthetic demands on the art-form itself. This Fourth World art is now in a continuous state of change and the attendant dynamics have created new forms at the same time that the process contains within it the potential emergence of still newer forms. As Graburn states:

The study of Fourth World arts is, par excellence, the study of *changing* arts — of emerging ethnicities, modifying identities, and commercial and colonial stimuli and repressive actions.[35]

Sources of change incorporated into commercial arts[36] come from both without and within, according to the tastes of the buyers and the efforts of the producers.[37]

Handmade basketry has become a marketable commodity, a development recognized by the producers, stemming as it does largely from the appreciation of a new and broader constituency — the Western consumer.

Fig. 43 Braided sweet green grass flared bowls, *seroto*, Basotho. Seqoqong village, kingdom of Lesotho, southern Africa. August 1977.

Among the Zulu, there has been a tremendous upsurge in basketry production due, in large part, to the efforts of a few key figures. Home-craft groups have long been in existence in KwaZulu, but there was typically no co-ordination, quality control, or marketing apparatus. In 1972, members of Zulu churches in KwaZulu, formed a central organization, the Vukani Association, meaning 'get up and go' or 'wake up', to encourage, guide, and assist existing church handicraft organizations, as well as to foster new home-craft groups in previously unorganized areas.[38] The man responsible for co-ordinating this association, for organizing successful exhibitions in Europe, and for promoting their marketing is Reverend Kjell Lofroth, a Swedish pastor. Working closely with Zulu co-ordinators and buyers, his efforts have ensured the production of basketry of quality and innovative decoration. Under his direction, a carefully managed marketing effort, that has preserved the quality of Zulu basketry produced in carefully controlled numbers, continues to maintain their attraction as much sought-after objects for the collector's market. In addition, Gatsha Buthelezi, statesman and honorary hereditary chief of the Zulu, has taken an interest in the art-form and, as a collector, seeks to ensure the survival of this traditional art.

As previously suggested, in this period of revival there has been a modification of forms to satisfy developing commercial needs. Perhaps the most

65

Fig. 44 Selection of high-quality competition baskets, Bayei. Gomare village, Ngamiland, Botswana. July 1982.

striking change to typify recent Zulu basketry is the emerging emphasis of design and colourful decoration. European sources, missionaries, United Nations workers, and collectors in North America have stimulated this creative innovation, encouraging the weavers to enlarge and elaborate on their traditional designs. The Europeans, for example, have not suggested actual designs, but rather simply suggested that Zulu weavers decorate their baskets more fully.[39] Quick to adapt new ideas to their traditional methods, the Zulu incorporate greater diversity of design, colour, and textural weaving technique to produce the most desired baskets of southern Africa.

They have also answered the demand for previously nonexistent pieces sought by the Western market. Zulu weavers use their traditional coiling technique to construct large, cylindrical containers to serve as planters. In addition, round and oval trays of different sizes, and sets of rectangular table-mats are made to adorn Western homes. Throughout, quality has not only been maintained but improved, and the artisans themselves take pride in their work and the continuance of a valued tribal tradition.

The Bayei and Hambukushu response to Western demand has been vibrant, like that of the Zulu, at the same time that the forces of the market-place are exacting a price, a decline in the overall quality of their basketry.

In 1970, with the assistance of Peace Corps volunteers, the Botswanacraft Marketing Company was formed as a trust by the Botswana government. The aims were to stimulate the production of the traditional crafts of the Bayei and Hambukushu, and to provide a market for authentic rural handicrafts. Since then, the United Nations International Trade Centre has assisted Botswanacraft and played an instrumental role in creating an international interest in these local crafts.[40] At the same time, the United Nations Development Program in Botswana has instructed local handicraft developers to travel to villages to purchase baskets so that woven objects can be brought out of remote areas. It has encouraged the construction of baskets of higher quality,

66

those that are firm and tightly woven, and seeks to exercise quality control in purchasing baskets.[41] Competitions have been organized to stimulate the weavers to produce well-constructed, decorative articles. (Fig. 44) Thus, a concerted effort has been made by Europeans to encourage the Bayei and Hambukushu weavers to maintain their age-old tradition. An export market now flourishes to the extent that the demand for good quality baskets exceeds the supply.

But this demand, the result of the very success of their broad-based marketing effort, is having a negative impact, is in fact sabotaging their tradition. Quality control is virtually non-existent as they flood the market with baskets of increasing inferiority to satisfy the insatiable demand their marketing efforts have created. Typical of unsophisticated Fourth World people, the nuances of the market-place are lost to them as they substitute quantity for the carefully controlled production of high-quality work.

As we have seen, the response of the basket-making peoples of southern Africa to acculturation and the lure of Western values and life-styles has been marked by diversity, encompassing the entire spectrum from rejuvenation to extinction. Yet, while new influences may jeopardize tradition, they have, in turn, stimulated creativity. A typically Western aspect of the market-place, market segmentation, has occurred. Today, the craftspeople gear their production to three distinct populations. Villagers continue to produce wares to meet the functional requirements dictated by their life-style, while the remaining two populations are, however, subgroups of the Western market. For the tourist, who may lack an appreciation of the indigenous culture, the artisans have brought contemporary themes to their work. For the collector, traditional product as authentic icon of the culture is produced. The craftspeople have been successful in fulfilling the requirements necessary to satisfy the taste of each population as suggested by the following breakdown by Graburn:

The objects produced must have artistic and ethnographic value in order to attract the attention of overseas art buyers, some national value in order to attract the support of buyers from the dominant society, and some traditional value to attract native patronage.[42]

Thus, an African craft that began with functional intent has become an artistic medium that is increasingly motivated by aesthetics. Although it cannot be denied that there has been a Western influence on basket making, the art-form itself has not changed because traditional techniques continue to be used. The fact that the artisan can differentiate between and satisfy varied consumer needs does not detract from the craft; rather it reflects a new level of sophistication and expertise in a contemporary world. Yet, the risks attending these developments persist.

With commercial success comes the loss of interest in producing the traditional, as commercial exploitation and resulting monetary gain reward the artisans by financing their purchases of modern man-made objects. The danger is that the traditional, internal arts will become purely external arts, those made essentially for the Western market, and that the traditional art,

67

the initial source of attraction, may disappear. In turn, modern agricultural techniques may loosen and destroy the incentive to produce traditional articles as monetary reward encourages the people to spend their time in more remunerative enterprises.

Finally, short-sighted and ineffective marketing—distribution which creates a glut of poorer-quality articles—could undermine the collective value of the objects. There remains the danger that the market could disappear through a combination of price increases that effectively price the baskets out of the market. Finally, as people are drawn to the cities from rural areas, the pool of available talent to whom the skill must be taught for the tradition to continue, may diminish and ultimately disappear altogether.

Thus, we have before us a scenario marked by a tragic paradox. Western appreciation and its attendant commercialization which, on the one hand, forestalls the disappearance of a once-vibrant, living tradition, inexorably endangers and forever alters the art-form which, in its beauty and authenticity, carries within it the contradictory seeds of preservation and extinction.

3 Pottery:
A Dying Tradition

It might be expected that pottery, an eminently functional and ceremonial art, would continue to be a vibrant art-form among the tribes of southern Africa. Yet, their traditional pottery is on the decline, falling victim to the direct impact of acculturation. Unlike the interest basketry has engendered in the Western market, tribal pottery, probably largely because of its inherent qualities of fragility and relative paucity of decoration, has not captured the collector's or tourist's eye. Without this mitigating factor, pottery production suffers increasingly from competition with mass-produced utensils which have become available in even the most remote areas.

Yet, as in the case of basketry, as acculturation has affected each tribe's life-style, their pottery traditions have accordingly responded, respecting individual characteristics of habitat, ecology, and location. This once flourishing craft, the work of the women, except in the Okavango River areas where the Hambukushu men are the potters, has continued to diminish in practice to the point that today we cannot discuss Bayei pottery because it no longer exists. While the Basotho and Hambukushu maintain a faltering pottery tradition, as in the case of basketry, it is that of the Zulu which continues to lead an existence albeit a threatened one, midwifed by a few dedicated individuals. While a comparison of museum examples with those pots currently produced reveals that, unlike basketry, form, technique and decoration have remained the same, the change lies in the decreasing number of practising potters and the growing substitution of machine-made products.

Meyerowitz in his 1936 article, 'A Report on the Possibility of the Development of Village Crafts in Basutoland', briefly discussed Basotho pottery considering function as well as materials used and methods employed. Even at this early date, he feared the harmful influence Westernization would have on their arts and crafts, implying that this external influence would rob the work of its uniqueness and creativity. In fact, Westernization has more than robbed their work of its artistic character since the very existence of the tradition is currently threatened.

Woman's work, pots are most generally created to serve utilitarian household purposes. The Basotho construct the *nkho* to carry and store water, and the *morifi* and *moritsoana*, respectively the larger and smaller beer pots, also used for storing small quantities of grain. They drink from the *likona* and eat porridge from the *mopotjoana* and *lefitsoana* which are employed for other purposes as well.[43] Although some pots are decorated with engraved lines

Following pages: above left, Fig. 47 Nesta Nala prepares good clay, *i-bumba,* Zulu. Ndondondware village, KwaZulu, South Africa,. July 1981; *below left,* Fig. 48 Nesta Nala wedges the clay on her grinding stone, *itshe,* Zulu. Nondondondware village, Kwa-Zulu, South Africa. July 1981; *above right,* Fig. 49 A clay coil ready to become a pot, Zulu. Ndondondware village, KwaZulu, South Africa. July 1981; *below right,* Fig. 50 Nesta Nala moulds and smooths the pot's surface, Zulu. Ndondondware village, KwaZulu, South Africa. July 1981.

69

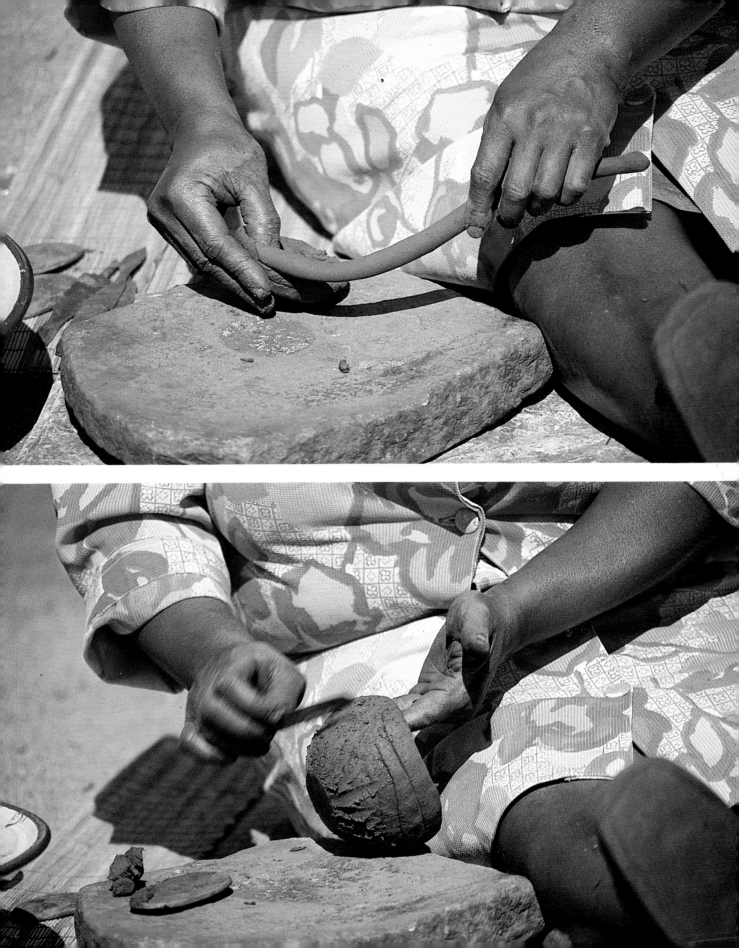

Fig. 45 Potter, *moka-komba*, employing coiling technique, Hambukushu. Kwegudi, Ngamiland, Botswana. 1969. *Courtesy of Thomas Larson.*

and painted with ochres and other substances, generally the pots remain un-embellished as can be readily noted in the above examples.

Traditionally, the pot's price was set by the amount of grain equal to the pot's capacity, but even this tradition has changed in favour of cash exchange. Mr Meyerowitz was correct in his prediction, in that pottery has all but become an art of the Basotho past.

Among the Hambukushu, pottery is the art of the men, the potter being referred to as a *mokakomba,* one who specializes in constructing large beer pots, *kandimbe.* (Fig. 45) Creating their pottery pieces from clay that is moulded into rolls, their pot is dried in the sun for a week before firing, a fifteen-minute process. Once the *kandimbe* is completed, a bulb-shaped beer basket is plaited over the pot. Two sets of elements made of strong reeds, *matete,* which are slit down one side, opened and flattened, and which cross each other at right angles alternately passing over and under each other, pro-

Fig. 46 Plaited basket woven over clay beer pot, *kandimbe*, Hambukushu. Etsha village, Nagamiland, Botswana. August 1977.

Following pages: above left, Fig. 51 Nesta Nala moulds and smooths the pot's surface, Zulu. Ndondondware village, Kwa-Zulu, South Africa. July 1981; *below left,* Fig. 52 Nesta Nala arranges aloe and wood over the pots for their first firing process, Zulu. Ndondondware village, KwaZulu, South Africa. July 1981; *above right,* Fig. 53 Glossy black surface attained by rubbing fired pot surface with gooseberry leaves, Zulu. Ndondondware village, KwaZulu, South Africa. July 1981; *below right,* Fig. 54 Strainer, stirrer, pot cover, *imbenge,* and beer pot, *ukhamba,* required for the serving and drinking of beer, Zulu. Eshowe, KwaZulu, South Africa. February 1982.

duce a chequer-board effect. This plaited basket frequently remains as an outer covering for the pot. (Fig. 46)

Larson's 1975 work noted that pot making along the Okavango River continued to thrive because of demand for the *kandimbe*.[44] Yet, a mere five years later, this author found that handmade pots were being rapidly replaced by metal, plastic, and enamel products.

Zulu pottery making possesses a long history and today small numbers of Zulu women continue the tradition. In fact, Zulu pot making today must be reduced to a consideration of individuals, persons intent on keeping this fragile tradition alive. It is to a consideration of Nesta Nala we now turn. A master Zulu potter, she lives in Ndondondware, a village of 3 000 inhabitants, nestled into a mountainside in the heart of KwaZulu. One of the few who remain of Zulu potters, she is striving to improve and perfect an art-form even as it is endangered by the effects of Westernization.

Nesta Nala lives in the traditional setting of an integrated Zulu village that consists of huts clustered in circular arrangements deep in central KwaZulu or 'Place of Heaven'. This rural Zulu area's economy is based on standard agricultural pursuits, crop cultivation and cattle raising. The division of labour is clear-cut, the men tending the animals and clearing and cultivating the fields, while the women run the households and maintain the craft traditions of bead-work,[45] basketry,[46] and pottery.

The art of pottery has a long history among the Zulu[47] and it is the women who are the masters of this utilitarian craft. In this rural locale where the potter's wheel is unknown, the technique of coiling symmetrical pots in various shapes and sizes is a tradition that has been passed down from one generation to the next, although today Westernization's effects have spread to even the most remote KwaZulu villages and plastic, enamel, and other manufactured containers are now replacing traditional pottery, threatening its continued existence. However, forty-two-year-old Nesta Nala continues the tradition, exhibiting an unusual degree of talent, skill, and determination. Having learned the craft from her mother, Siphiwe Nala, she is proud to share her artistry.

The process of fashioning pottery vessels begins when Nesta gathers good clay, referred to as *ibumba,* from the mountainside, combining red and dark clays with sherds. (Fig. 47) This clay is ground to a fine powder on a grinding stone, an *itshe,* and is then mixed with water to create the degree of plasticity necessary. (Fig. 48) Next, she wedges the composition and it remains in this form until she feels it is ready for coiling. Once the raw materials have been gathered and prepared, the task of fashioning the pottery begins.

Nesta begins by flattening a lump of wet clay which forms the disc-like base of the pot. This disc is placed on a small wreath of dried grass, *inkatha,* a grinding stone. (Fig. 49) She adds coils of increasing lengths, building up the walls of the vessel and pinching them into position until the pot has reached its intended size and shape. Giving careful attention to symmetry, form, and the thinness of the walls, she smooths both the inner and outer walls with pieces of calabash, a stone, or metal tools. (Figs. 50, 51) With this basic construction process completed, she covers the pots with blankets and places them inside the hut for one to two days. They are returned outside to dry for another seven days before the firing process, which is usually done during fine weather in the afternoon.

For the first firing, Nesta Nala arranges dry aloe and wood over the pots which have been placed in a shallow pit. (Fig. 52) The pots are burnished to a mottled, leather-like brown surface and remain in the embers until the fire has been completely extinguished. Pots which are intended for storage or cooking remain in this state, while those articles intended for eating and drinking undergo another firing process utilizing cakes of dry cow dung. During this second process, the fire must become red-hot after which it is smothered with powdered dung. As a result, these pots emerge possessing a black surface which is then rubbed with gooseberry leaves, a small flattened stone, *imbokode,* (Fig. 53), and animal fat. This final rubbing process gives a glossy black finish to the pottery.

Fig. 57 Drinking pot, *ukhamba*, used for sour milk and beer (back right); urn-shaped vessel for liquids, *uphiso* (back left); small drinking pots, *umancishane* (foreground) Zulu. *Courtesy of Abe Frajndlich.*

Fig. 59 Drinking pot, *umansishane*, featuring incised decoration (foreground); clay pellets, *amasumpa*, embellish pot surface (back right) Zulu. *Courtesy of Abe Frajndlich.*

Fig. 55 Woman bearing beer storage pot, *iphangela*, on her head, Zulu. Eshowe, KwaZulu, South Africa. September 1979.

Opposite page: above, Fig. 56 Nesta Nala with her collection of completed pots, *ukhamba*, Zulu. Ndondondware village, KwaZulu, South Africa. July 1981; *below,* Fig. 58 Woman serving beer to her husband, demonstrating respectful attitude, *hlonipha,* from beer pots covered by traditional beaded *imbenge,* Zulu. Eshowe, KwaZulu, South Africa. February 1982.

78

The shapes and sizes of traditional pottery vary according to function. The preparation and consumption of beer requires implements and serving-pieces to fulfil the requirements of a custom that is both daily routine and ceremonial. (Fig. 54) Sorghum-derived beer, *utshwala,* is the Zulu's national beverage and refreshes not only the living, but is offered to ancestral spirits in homage as proof the dead have not been forgotten. In addition, legend says that each springtime during the feast of the Chieftainess of the Skies or Goddess of the Grain, Nomkhubulwana visits earth expecting to find small pots of beer brewed especially for her by the young maidens who till the land.[48] To encourage the goddess to ensure bountiful crops, the family offers her small pots of their brewed beer, the result of a process that requires a variety of implements.

The largest of the traditional pots is the undecorated *imbiza,* a vessel used for cooking and capable of holding up to 40 litres of fermented *utshwala,* the sorghum-derived traditional beer. A slightly smaller pot is the *iphangela,* (Fig. 55) while Nesta Nala prefers making the *ukhamba,* a large spherical pot without a neck which can contain 20 litres of liquid and is used for serving beer at large gatherings and festivals. (Fig. 56) Since these pots and their contents symbolize hospitality, those used for entertaining guests are invariably decorated to enhance their beauty. The Zulu incise decoration into the surface of their pots using zigzag, arc, cross-hatch, triangle, and diamond motifs. Diamond and triangular designs predominate, while pots embellished with up-ended triangles signal that the men alone may use them since the triangle is a male symbol.[49]

She also makes a smaller *ukhamba,* the customary drinking pot from which visitors imbibe beer and sour milk, the symbols of hospitality, (Fig. 57, back right) and the *uphiso,* an urn-shaped vessel with a cylindrical funnel which prevents spillage and facilitates pouring. (Fig. 57, back left)

A pot similar to but smaller than the *ukhamba* is the *umancishane.* The word *ncisha,* from which its name is derived, signifies 'to be stingy'[50] and when beer is served in this container, it may indicate that the guest should simply visit for a short period, drink his beverage and leave, or that the host is short of beer. (Fig. 57, foreground) Upon receiving the *umancishane,* the visitor generally realizes its implications.

Beer pots do not complete the collection of pieces required to observe Zulu custom because, 'beer must be covered to protect it not only from insects but from spells caused by the depositing of evil medicine.'[51] The beer pot cover, *imbenge,* is a saucer-shaped bowl woven from ilala palm leaf, and traditionally beaded when used for entertaining guests. (Fig. 58) The *imbenge* has three functions: to serve as a cover for the traditional globular clay pot, *ukhamba,* when it is filled with beer; to be used as a container for serving food; or to function as a plate for the beer stirrer, *uhashu,* skimmer, *isiketho,* and gourd to rest on during the serving of beer.

Beaded *imbenge,* regarded as treasured articles, are stored in the main hut of the compound and brought out when guests are entertained. The pot covers, used purely as utilitarian objects inside the hut, are usually plain and unembellished, and are allocated to the women. Each family has a host of pot covers, since every male member of the household owns his own beaded cover. The heavily beaded *imbenge*, with predominantly white beads and some colour motifs, are typical of those to be found among a girl's dowry or which are given as wedding gifts by a bride to her prospective groom or father-in-law.

As noted earlier, it is function that determines the decoration of Zulu pottery. Vessels used for storage and cooking remain plain, smooth, and undecorated, while those used for serving or drinking are decorated with different motifs to enhance their beauty. (Fig. 59) The two main techniques of decorating Zulu pottery, incising and attaching groups of small clay pellets, *amasumpa*, result in varied designs. In the former, Nesta Nala, using a metal tool, comb, or stick, incises various motifs on the soft clay of the unfired pot. The graphic patterns range from diamond, triangular, and V-shapes with cross-hatched lines, to arcs, semicircles and floral patterns which are usually incised around the belly of the pot. Using the technique of arranging small warts of clay, *amasumpa*, on the surface of the pots, she obtains the sculptured effect of lozenges, curves, rectangular blocks, and bands around the vessels. This traditional method of raised decoration is mirrored by the work of men carvers in their manufacture of wooden objects like head-rests, milk pails, meat trays, and eating spoons.

Unfortunately, unlike the prolific and talented Nesta Nala, we have noted that Zulu pottery as a whole is on the decline. In contrast to the renaissance Zulu basketry is currently enjoying[52] because organizations and markets have been established to foster this art, pottery has not been adopted in like manner, in part because its fragility hampers shipping, it is less decorative, and it continues to enjoy little more than a local market. The small market that does exist may well diminish as more in rural areas break with tradition and resort to commercial alternatives. One among the very few women involved in constructing traditional Zulu pottery, Nesta Nala, who is truly devoted to preserving a significant segment of her culture, has not ventured into new forms nor succumbed to the pressures of change. Like her mother, Siphiwe Nala, from whom she learned her art, Nesta Nala has passed on this vanishing tradition to her daughter, Bongekile Nala, who, it is hoped, will be one of an increasing number of potters to pass the art-form on to the next generation.

4 Dress and Ornament:
A Means of Communication

The traditions of dress and bodily adornment practised by the tribal peoples of southern Africa have a rich history since this very visual expression frequently symbolizes values and cultural traditions while fulfilling functional and decorative requirements. As is the case with their other material traditions and perhaps to an even greater extent, this societal and individual mode of communication reflects shifting values and notions of beauty as it continues to evolve under the impact of Westernization. Always susceptible to individual variation, customary tribal expressions—their styles and meanings— are affected increasingly by acculturation as both individual and discernible tribal patterns of modification find their way into the clothing and body ornament of the people.

Among the Zulu, Basotho, Bayei, Hambukushu, and Herero there exist visually distinctive modes of adornment that now, more than ever, mirror the effects of change. Cultural expressions that have frequently remained unchanged for centuries have been dramatically modified into extinction or exist tenuously in competition with more desirable Western styles. At the very least, the two, the traditional and modern, may exist side by side as individual expression makes its mark on long-established customs of adornment, whose roles as social regulator and cultural value transmitter are increasingly challenged by the evolution of this highly communicative form.

The bead-work tradition is common to the black peoples of southern Africa, and has ritual, economic, and social significance. Among the Zulus who possess a distinctive national dress and elaborate ornamental tradition, special emphasis is placed on social relationships, as the symbolism of dress and bead-work mark the values and the stages of social development through which the individual passes. Groupings determined by age, sex, marital, and kinship status prevail, and the dress and bead configurations worn attest to one's appropriate group affiliation. From ancient times, bits of bone, horn, shells, polished wood fragments and animal claws have been pierced and strung to fashion necklaces and belts. Zulu dress, then, is culturally regulated so that one's status may be readily determined. Attaching particular meaning to colours, unlike the other tribes, for example, only a girl who has not reached puberty may wear a white cloth around her body since white symbolizes purity. While interpretation of any particular piece is often very individual, some principles which underlie the colour code have been determined. Although when a Zulu engages in interpretation he appears to arrive

Opposite page: above, Fig. 60 Young maidens displaying traditional love-letters, Zulu. KwaZulu, South Africa. February 1980; *below left,* Fig. 64 Married woman displaying typical wooden ear-plug, Zulu. Tugela Ferry, Kwa-Zulu, South Africa. November 1979; *below right,* Fig. 67 Manufactured scarves adorn traditional head-dress, Zulu. Tugela Ferry, KwaZulu, South Africa. June 1980.

at a spontaneous, almost automatic, response, the Westerner, more accustomed to linguistic procedures of translation, requires rudimentary guidelines like the following: 1) *colour matching preferences* reflect colour selection and rejection of beads strung next to one another; 2) *rules of arrangement* determine how various colours are ordered by pre-arranged sequence; 3) *type selection* regulates those specific colours pre-selected for specific types of articles.[53]

While Zulu bead-work consists of a number of types including simple strings of beads, largely flat constructions with multiple strands of beads attached at the corners, single or multiple beaded ropes used as girdles, bead-work-covered objects like sticks, gourds and dolls, and clothing like skirts and shawls typically of leather, it is their love-letter, *ubala abuyise,* meaning 'one writes in order that the other should reply', the existence of which is unique to them, that is threatened by change.[54] This most symbolic Zulu bead-work is a private and public communication of the status of one's love life. Because they had possessed no written language, much of their communication took this visual form. Using beads imported and made from local materials, women of every stratum have made love-letters, simple strings of beads worn around the neck or about the head which feature several favourite colours—probably those most easily obtainable from the trading posts. To the Zulu, the white bead means love and purity; black is darkness, difficulty, and misfortune; green signifies sickness; yellow symbolizes wealth; blue means happiness, and red is the red from sore eyes which have looked in vain for their lover.[55]

In spite of these noted general similarities in colour symbolism, precise interpretation can be made solely by one who knows the specific local origin of the love-letter and the colour code native to it, because an ambiguity of meaning continues to pervade translation. Field-work evidence attests to the ingenuity of the Zulu in conveying personal messages via a medium giving each bead worker an individual idiolect that is susceptible to translation by local native informants alone. In fact, of the previously noted colours frequently employed, only white possesses a consistent message. White beads of bone, *ithambo,* or milk, *ubisi,* always convey a positive message: love, purity, goodness, happiness, virginity, or good luck. For black, green, pink, yellow, blue, and red beads, there are several interpretations, which generally fall into two categories, those of either positive or negative content. For instance, black beads, *isitimane,* most frequently mean darkness, gloom, disappointment, or sorrow, but they are also used to represent a very dark-skinned person or the kaross, the symbol of marriage.[56] (Fig. 60)

Having used large numbers of beads for approximately 120 years, it is the young girls who have resorted to 'writing' beaded love-letters to the men they love. Zulu men, in turn, proudly display them, wearing them all over their heads, necks, and chests, greater numbers signifying greater numbers of wives or lovers in a reflection of wealth and status. In addition, men will enlist their sisters' skill in producing an appropriate love-letter destined for the female of their affection. Characteristic of all is a complexity of pattern, the combinations of which have symbolic meaning as previously suggested.

While the most predominant motif is the triangle, intricacy of pattern is

84

Fig. 61 Variety of geometric patterns characteristic of bead-work, Zulu. *Courtesy of the Africana Museum, Johannesburg, South Africa.*

Following page: Fig. 62 Married women's flared red-ochred head-dress, Zulu. Tugela Ferry, Kwa-Zulu, South Africa. November 1979.

obtained by geometric designs of diamonds, chevrons, and zigzags, as well. Patterns obtain their particular character from the alternation of small oval units of colour much like a brick wall, while the mosaic-like texture of their vibrant colours enhances the beauty of the bead-work. (Fig. 61) Although the

Fig. 63 Beaded headband conveying message of social importance, Zulu. Tugela Ferry, KwaZulu, South Africa. December 1980.

87

method of threading with fine gut somewhat limits shape variation, triangles, straight lines, zigzags, and small squares made of blocks of four or nine beads, are common.[57]

In addition to the selection of beads of particular colour, bead workers can juxtapose beads differently to produce varied messages, and more beads of appropriate colour are added to emphasize a point since the relative proportions of various colours found in an object may inflect the meaning.[58] For instance, one item described by Mrs Twala features beads in the following order: yellow, black, pink, lavender blue, pink, black, and yellow. Since Zulu love-letters convey a message, the *ucu,* read consecutively beginning with the bead nearest the top, the interpretation of this message *inkosozana phakathi kwemfinbinga* is, 'The man no longer loved me. When he died he had already rejected me'. However, Mrs Twala explains, had the order of the colours been reversed, the message would have been, 'When he died I had already rejected him'.[59] Thus, the bead love-letters the Zulu maiden makes and gives her young man convey her feelings about their relationship.[60]

Once married, the woman dons the distinctive flared head-dress to indicate her changed status. (Fig. 62) One of the most distinctive African tribal hair-styles worn in the Tugela Ferry-Durban region, it is a beehive-like head-dress of elaborate construction. Fig leaves are used to plait the hair into long spikes which are fitted tightly over a typical flared tin plate which is smeared with red clay, forming a semi-permanent head-dress when dry.[61] Bead-work on the head-dress conveys messages about her virginity before marriage, her feelings toward her in-laws, whether or not she has borne children and the type of marriage in which she is involved. (Fig. 63) Married women alone may wear this article.

With the approach of marriage, the girl may wear the *isicholo,* the topknot which distinguishes a married woman. The hair is straightened by plaiting it with grass into long tendrils after which the hairs of the crown are sewn together and greased with a sour milk and red ochre mixture while the rest of the head is shaved. Compared to those of the past, larger topknots are worn today and a process of building the knot into a high conical mass is common enough that it often reaches a full 45 centimetres from the crown.

Bead-work jewellery marks the stages through which the Zulu passes from childhood to adulthood, as well. Ear-piercing, *qhumbuza*, marks the first of these and must be accomplished prior to puberty. Taking place at either the full or new moon, in the case of the former it is said that the children are made full—full members of the family—while in the latter instance, it is time to commence making a person, to add a new unit to the family.[62] In adulthood, large ear-plugs are worn by both Zulu men and women. (Fig. 64) Barbara Tyrell, an expert on Zulu folklore, explains that, according to ancestral custom, the ears are ritually pierced in childhood to ensure 'that the ears of the mind might also hear.'[63] Therefore, a Zulu adult with unpierced ears is ridiculed as having the comprehension of a child.

The information conveyed by Zulu bead-work covers a far wider range than that which is expressed by analogous symbols (engagement rings and wedding bands) in Western culture, while the prominence of interpersonal relationships in their lives is demonstrated. This visual language is, in any

88

event, dying out and more subtle messages like those of the past are increasingly not comprehended. At the same time, modern lettering is frequently to be found on the love-letters, replacing traditional geometric motifs as exposure to the West broadens tribal awareness of the outside world. (Fig. 60)

While bead-work is an essential component of Zulu dress, it fulfils by no means all their clothing requirements, as a diverse array of garments are employed in a colourful admixture of the old and new. Bright coloured garments in combination with bead-work suggest the juxtaposition of the traditional and modern in the costume of the Zulu of today. (Fig. 65) Here the typical skirt is topped by a modern undergarment over which is placed a traditional cape constructed of a fabric that appears to be particularly popular among the women. Beaded jewellery adorns the neck, wrists, and waist, while the outfit is finished off by Argyle socks and tennis shoes. (Fig. 66) What more fitting example of acculturated dress might one find?

To the traditional draped plate-like head-dress into which their hair is pulled is frequently added plastic barrettes of modern manufacture, while scarves of many colours are increasingly covering the ochred finish of yesterday. (Figs. 67, 68) Among the unmarried women, modern articles are now worn over machine-made hair nets as plastic headbands substitute for traditional beaded headbands as may be readily seen by comparing Figures 69, 70, and 71. In Figure 69, a modern plastic headband is placed in unconventional position on the head in contrast to the traditionally coloured beaded head ornament of Figure 71 and the circular beaded head decoration of Figure 70. At this time, it is a rare occurrence to find a Zulu accoutred in entirely traditional costume as a hybrid form of personal expression now characterizes their dress, although a poignant custom among educated urban Zulu women has developed. For special occasions, she may shun Western dress, donning the

89

Fig. 65 Traditional bead-work complemented by cape of contemporary fabric which replaces traditional skin garment, Zulu. Tugela Ferry, KwaZulu, South Africa. June 1980.

90

Fig. 66 Traditional bead-work displayed with modern undergarments, socks, shoes, and favoured cape, Zulu. Tugela Ferry, Kwa-Zulu, South Africa. June 1980.

91

full regalia of traditional Zulu costume in proud display of her cultural heritage.

Distinctive to the Basotho people and continuing practices among them are the use of blankets for dress and the tradition of initiating the girls, the *bale*, to adulthood. The effects of Christianity threaten the initiation school's existence however, while education has awakened Basotho interest in Western styles and garb.

Held during the summer months, the initiation school maintains traditional tribal values of Basotho society and in so doing, requires the wearing of a traditional costume that distinguishes this custom. Wearing hand-woven reed masks (Fig. 72) often decorated with glass beads and hand-rolled clay beads made by the older women of the village, the girls' faces and bodies are covered with white clay to signify their spiritual and physical separation from the community until the end of a ceremony lasting several months. (Fig. 73)

In addition, they wear leather cowhide skirts and eight or more hoops of grass rings around their waists. These rings have no beginning and no end so that evil cannot enter.[64] Bare-breasted, carrying forked, medicinally treated sticks, in daylight from the specially built house at the village edge where initiation to the rite of fertility and preparation for marriage takes place, the girls venture into the countryside. Any onlooker they encounter is wise to present them with a gift of money unless he or she wishes to risk being battered by the girls who use their forked-tipped sticks for this purpose.

In the evenings, they watch for the coming of the new moon, and it is at this time that the blankets which are worn during the early stages of initiation are cast off and the girls rush to the river where the matrons of the village greet them. By the time the girls have left the river's edge, their childhoods have been washed away and now that they are adults, they wear leaves, the *mabululo*. Borne by the matrons on their backs, they return home whereupon their bodies are covered with black powder, *pilo*, which is later replaced by a white clay called *phepa*.[65] While this annual initiation ceremony for young girls is still practised in remote villages in many parts of Lesotho, the practice has been discontinued due to the influence of missionaries, the church, and the literacy this exposure has wrought.

The Basotho blanket of today forms the bridge, albeit a threatened one, between the skin clothing made from wild and domestic animals worn prior to the mid-1800s, and modern dress. Before the discovery and exploitation of the Kimberley diamond-fields in the 1870s, the Basotho wore their traditional skin karosses, although the enhanced purchasing power that resulted, and the Basotho move to the mountains and its attendant game scarcity, led to increased reliance on the manufactured. Any skins available, after increasingly infrequent slaughters, were invariably used for shields, special garb, or trade, and were supplanted by wool or cotton blankets which were worn over corduroy trousers—a fashion that became so successful that even before 1900 specially designed blankets for the Basotho were being made by English firms like Wormald and Walker of Drewsbury.[66] British soldiers on campaign in the area had brought with them their regimental blankets which incorporated heraldic motifs with vividly coloured stripes in a horizontal design measuring 152 centimetres. The Basotho appropriated these blankets when possible and began wearing them, turning the stripes so that they appeared vertically.

In 1885, the Fraser Brothers Company sent a leopard kaross sewn on a skin foundation to a manufacturing company in Yorkshire, England, at the same time that drawings of decorated tribal huts were also submitted. A blanket simulating a leopard skin was produced, and by 1887, the 'Queen Victoria' blanket, named after their patron and protector, was created by the Fraser Brothers to commemorate the queen's diamond jubilee. This most popular of blankets reflected the improvement in quality as wool and mohair replaced traditional cotton, and brighter colours replaced the dull colours of their predecessors. Other motifs, tartan patterns of English origin and those inspired by hut designs, as well as a blanket called the *moholobela,* meaning 'to make a lot of noise', were created for weddings and other special occasions, as red proved to be the most popular colour. With increased demand came keener competition and the production of more attractive designs resulted. Yet fashion differed from one locale to another, and among the clans themselves, patterns and colours in demand in one area might have no attraction for the people of another.

As in the past, today the Basotho wear blankets in the winter for warmth (Fig. 74) and in the summer for relief from the heat. Fashions in blankets continue to vary particularly with respect to sex and age-determined tastes. (Fig. 75) So, too, does the manner in which the blanket is worn vary since the man pins the blanket on the right shoulder leaving his right arm free (Fig. 76), while the female fastens the blanket in the middle of her bosom. Bright colours—turquoise, red, and orange—are common, although more subtle colourations like greys and blacks, earth colours, and combinations of bright and subtle may find their way into blanket design. Patterned blankets of pastel colours, however, appear to be those most favoured by women. (Fig. 77)

History continues to creep into designs as symbols depicting current events, like the English crown and sceptre commemorating Queen Elizabeth's recent visit to Lesotho, as well as symbols of war, like aeroplanes and army badges, can be found. A young man faced with tendering the bride-price, *lobola,* to the father of his intended often informs the father that this suitor has a collection of expensive and attractive blankets which may include the chequered blanket, a highly regarded status symbol. Special blankets may be ordered for royal weddings, funerals, Independence Day, and political activities, and as a result, over 3 000 designs have been produced.[67]

A favoured design is that of the 'Lesotho' blanket featuring a crocodile, the symbol totem animal of Moshoeshoe's Kwena tribe, and featuring a hand holding Freedom's torch over the Maluti Mountains which are pictured as a wrist. Featuring the symbolic animal of Lesotho, when they find their way into a store the blankets are immediately sold since they are so highly prized. Feather designs symbolize protection since it was tribute feathers traded to the Zulus which helped prevent Zulu and Basotho from warring against one another. Designs depicting their standard conical hat are found although on the whole buyers seem to be more concerned with colour than symbols.

93

Fig. 68 Manufactured scarves adorn traditional head-dress, Zulu. Tugela Ferry, KwaZulu, South Africa. June 1980.

94

Fig. 69 Variety of plastic articles replace traditional beaded ornament, Zulu. Tugela Ferry, KwaZulu, South Africa. June 1980.

95

Fig. 78 Maiden wears glass and ostrich shell beads on her traditional hair-style and beaded, geometric-patterned skirt, Hambukushu. *Courtesy of Thomas Larson.*

Opposite page: above, Fig. 70 Variety of plastic articles replace traditional beaded ornament, Zulu. Tugela Ferry, KwaZulu, South Africa. June 1980; *below,* Fig. 71 Modern hair net and traditional bead-work headband, Zulu. Tugela Ferry, Kwa-Zulu, South Africa. June 1980.

Today, the Basotho blanket tradition remains, although they are increasingly worn over modern dress usually taking the form of cotton prints, skirts with several petticoats and attached apron for the women, while shirts and trousers garb the men.

Evidence of traditional Bayei and Hambukushu dress is limited since they, especially, have adopted Western styles of dress. Matrilineal societies, both the Bayei and Hambukushu have, however, placed importance on the adornment of their women, and bead-work is the form this expression often takes. An elaborate ritual celebrating puberty initiates the girl into adulthood, an observance which is not complete until she has received all the appropriate jewellery she must wear at the completion of this month-long rite.[68]

The traditional, panelled, beaded skirts presented to Bayei and Hambukushu girls at puberty by their grandmothers and worn on special occasions, were typically decorated with geometric designs including triangular and diamond shapes, zigzags, parallel lines, and chevron patterns. (Fig. 78) Black and

white are often used in designs which are dramatic in their simplicity. Beads made from ostrich eggshell were formerly used to make belts, the wide bands of the leather aprons, *majambaro,* necklaces, and the ornaments in their artificial *coiffures,* until commercial beads were made available by the trading stores.[69] Imported commercial glass beads from Europe, mainly Czechoslovakia, are used for most bead-work today.

As noted earlier, however, the *majambaro* is rarely worn, if ever. The *mande,* a traditional, highly valued piece of jewellery, is very rare today as well, and those that exist have been handed down from one generation to the next, although some European imitation porcelain *mande* have been sold more recently. Although these artefacts are highly prized by the people themselves, as well as by museums and collectors, those articles made today primarily satisfy the commercial market and little remains of traditional Bayei and Hambukushu garb as the effects of acculturation have all but wiped out the dress of their past.

Living close to the Bayei and Hambukushu are the tall, stately Herero, cattle herders who settled in Botswana after the German-Herero War (1903–07) drove them from German South West Africa (today Namibia), although ancient belief says that the ancestors descended from the *omumborumbonga* tree to which they still pay homage.[70] Before the influence of the missionaries, the Herero went about practically naked, attired only in animal skins and ostrich eggshell beads. Those articles distinctive to the Herero of Ngamiland now, however, number several, and traditional costume continues to be worn among them, although like the other tribes, the practice is threatened by Westernization.

The influence of the Victorian era transmitted through German missionaries has structured their code of dress until recently. Today, the women's daily attire consists of a multicoloured patchwork dress (Fig. 79) of store-bought fabric, while each group possesses its own specially coloured ceremonial version, the whole topped by a matching head-dress. (Fig. 80) This style, often called Mother Hubbards, mimics those first worn by German women pioneers in the early 1800s even though it is quite unsuited to the tropical climate. Even so, the dress, *ohorokueva,* utilizes varied materials combined in a construction that makes each dress unique. Consisting of either a bodice with skirt or a one-piece dress, added to it are a headscarf like a turban, a shawl, an apron, a belt, three or four petticoats (sometimes as many as five or six), necklaces, and other jewellery. Occasionally, additional ornament like ribbons or ruffles are added to the blouse to resemble a Victorian yoke, while the long, leg-of-mutton sleeves are finished with lined cuffs and button-fastened wristbands.[71] The full skirt often requires at least 11 to 13 metres of material and is gathered at the waist flaring broadly at the bottom. Rows of brightly coloured beads swing freely from the bodice, favourites including diamond or cube-shaped beads made of soft, fragrant-smelling wood called *orupapa* which enhance the attractiveness of the woman since 'no woman should smell like a goat'.[72]

The petticoats worn underneath increase the skirt's volume enhancing the Herero's swaying stride, a mark of superior birth and breeding and a practice which stems from Herero ancestors who moved slowly because their legs

Fig. 83 Engraving depicting extinct traditional head-dress *ekori ro Vakazendu*, Herero. 1869. *Courtesy of the Africana Museum, Johannesburg, South Africa.*

99

Fig. 73 Clay-covered *bale* girls in traditional costume of hide skirts and grass hoops, Basotho. Near Roma, kingdom of Lesotho. November 1979.

Fig. 76 Traditional *poona* blanket fastened on right shoulder for flexibility of movement, Basotho. Kingdom of Lesotho, southern Africa. January 1976.

Opposite page: Fig 74 Manufactured woollen blankets draped about the shoulders and wrapped around the waist in traditional fashion, Basotho. Teyateyaneng, kingdom of Lesotho, southern Africa. September 1977.

100

Fig. 84 Twentieth-century version of the now extinct head-dress *ekori ro Vakazendu*, Herero. *Courtesy of the Africana Museum, Johannesburg, South Africa.*

102

Fig. 85 Women displaying traditional head-dress, Herero. *Courtesy of the Africana Museum, Johannesburg, South Africa.*

and arms were heavily weighted with brass rings, highly prized possessions. The skirt itself may be covered by an apron which is long for work (Fig. 81) but shortened and ornamented for dress. A thick leather or plastic belt covered in dress material and decorated with copper or a white metal medallion-shaped clasp, binds the waist, while a handmade or commercially produced shawl of light-weight, colourful material wraps the shoulders, except in the winter when heavier blanket material is used.

The costume is finished off frequently with jewellery including neck decorations of brass and copper wire, leather anklets, and rings that encircle the thigh just above the knee and ring the leg just below it. In addition, they wear 18-metre *morokuru* wood and ostrich eggshell necklaces carved by the men. The wood beads, *tawa*, are octagonal, and glass and enamel beads are frequently intermingled with them.

The Herero woman reveals her head to her husband alone, and she is, therefore, never seen in public without her scarf. A rectangular, flattened, padded top for height with two rolls or horns protruding from the front is the currently accepted head-dress (Fig. 82), although a particularly distinctive, now extinct, Herero head-dress with an intriguing past is the *ekori ro Vakazendu* (Fig. 83), a leather helmet which bears a striking resemblance to Viking headpieces as well as the archaic Greek *kredemnon.*[73] Consisting of a leather crown with a long fringe of scrap-iron beads that covers the head, three-pointed, leaf-shaped, parchment prongs decorated with perforations and twine stitching were sewn to the crown from which they rose vertically about 25 centimetres, as suggested by old lithographs (Fig. 84), although versions of the early 1900s were of a more refined and elongated shape. The highest points were set with beads of iron, while panels which covered the neck and extended to the small of the back were heavily worked with artistic beaded designs. The leather front-piece was sewn to the back and tightly rolled, framing the face.[74] (Fig. 85)

103

Fig. 75 Children sporting traditional woollen blankets, Basotho. Roma, kingdom of Lesotho, southern Africa. August 1977.

Opposite page: Fig. 79 Victorian-inspired multicoloured patchwork dress of manufactured cotton, Herero. Tsau village, Ngamiland, Botswana. August 1977.

Fig. 86 Pre-pubescent girls wear fringed leather loin-cloths, Herero. Tsau village, Ngamiland, Botswana. August 1977.

All but extinct among Herero men is their traditional dress, a simple, plaited leather belt worn around the waist to which a small apron strung with heavy iron beads is hung to protect it from movement or being blown away. In the back, attached to the same belt, is a moderately sized apron, while straps of long suspended strings decorate their knees. To complete this costume, a sheep- or goat-skin is draped over the shoulders.[75] This attire is not commonly seen today and, similarly, while the little girls still wear leather loincloths and skirts (Fig. 86), the young boys begin by wearing loincloths, later to graduate to Western clothes.

Since the Herero woman is a fine seamstress, not only does she enjoy making colourful patchwork dresses for herself, but dolls for her children as well. The most interesting quality of the doll is its witty character, capturing the individual nature of the Herero woman while its costumes represent various stages in a woman's life: pre-puberty, puberty, and adulthood, in addition to depicting ancestral dress. Hand-sewn with big, running stitches, they consist of a bodice attached to an ample skirt. (Fig. 87) These rag dolls are fashioned from old dress material such as cotton and twill, although no sewing is required to make the parts of the doll because the body is made of folded material which is wadded and bandaged with ribbons of torn cloth.

The figure possesses a faceless, hairless, coiffed head prolonged by an elongated neck, well-rounded breasts, an erect, thin torso, a pair of straight, handless arms, prominent buttocks, and a pair of straight, skinny legs with or without feet. The head is always small in relation to the rest of the body and is made of a wad of rags tightly covered with another piece of material. The buttocks are so out of proportion to the rest of the doll that they remind one

Fig. 87 Full-skirted tra-
ditionally costumed doll
mirroring typical female
garb, Herero. Tsau village,
Ngamiland, Botswana.
August 1977.

Following pages: left, Fig.
80 Matching head-dress
and shawl, Herero. Maun,
Botswana. August 1977;
right, Fig. 81 Functional
apron complementing tra-
ditional dress, Herero.
Tsau, Nagamiland, Bot-
swana. August 1977.

107

of the Bushmen women, especially since Maun, where most of the dolls are made, is situated on the fringe of the Kalahari Desert.

The Ngamiland rag doll has not changed over the last forty years except to reflect shifts in fashion. According to older women, the prominent dress and buttocks, as well as the very tightly bonneted blank face, have always been its remarkable features. This type of doll is the direct reflection of the women who are stately, aristocratic, and beautifully dressed in brightly coloured patchwork themselves. This handicraft will exist as long as Herero women maintain their traditional dress, but when styles change, it is likely that the dolls will, too. Unlike the Zulu love-letters, the Basotho *bale*, and the Bayei and Hambukushu bead-work, the Herero doll continues more than a marginal existence, a survivor for the present among a host of faltering southern African costume traditions.

Opposite page: Fig. 88 Children wearing loin-cloths, *ghabi*, Ndebele. KwaNdebele, South Africa. November 1980.

111

Fig. 77 Variety of colour and design typical of blankets, Basotho. Roma, kingdom of Lesotho, southern Africa. December 1975.

Fig. 82 Flattened rectangular head-dress with two frontal rolls, Herero. Tsau village, Ngamiland, Botswana. August 1977.

112

5 Distinctive Design:

Ndebele Bead-work and Mural Decoration

Of the tribal peoples of southern Africa, the Ndebele have produced an art long known for a vivid creativity featuring the successful adaptation and harmonious integration of outside influences. Since their artistic production is so pervasive a part of their culture, an investigation of their decorative arts is suggestive of their social patterns, values, preferences, and styles. Today, however, because of the widespread effects of Westernization, these social patterns, values, and preferences are undergoing ever more rapid change, and this process is having a direct effect on the styles of the art they produce as motifs and materials change and the symbolism behind the work shifts or is lost.

Bead-work is one of the oldest and most elemental of the decorative arts practised by the peoples of southern Africa and, among the Ndebele, it has markedly influenced an additional art-form for which they are noted, the decorative mural painting of their homes. Both forms possess significant cultural, ceremonial, and decorative aspects that are now changing at a pace that endangers their continued existence. In jeopardy is a bead-work tradition that tells the story of the Ndebele from infancy through death and a mural tradition that possesses artistic and ceremonial implications of wide-ranging cultural importance.

The Ndebele, among the smallest tribes in southern Africa,[76] are of Nguni descent and speak a dialect of Zulu. Their present location is KwaNdebele, an area defined by an imaginary triangle connecting Pretoria, Middelburg, and Marble Hall. While many facets of the Ndebele culture are revealed by the decorative arts, the women remain the sole practitioners and transmitters of an art that, by its very openness, seems to be life affirming. From birth until death, the story of an individual's life may be read in the composition of the beads that are worn.

The complexity of bead-work as cultural icon is apparent from the very first days of the individual, as the four to five-day-old infant, who, during a ceremony in which grandparents traditionally select a name, is adorned with a *khetsa*, a small beaded collar, constructed primarily of white beads. The child wears this initial necklace for approximately two years after which it is passed on to another child.

More specifically, a boy's birth is heralded by a ceremony in which the uncles beat the father with two beaded sticks, indicating that he has fathered a soldier, *lesole*. In the case of the birth of a girl, the mother's sisters fill

113

Fig. 89 Long strips of bead-work, *siyaya*, symbolize tears, Ndebele. KwaNdebele, South Africa. December 1980.

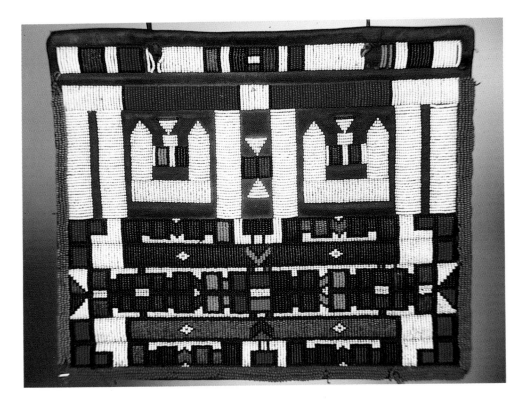

Fig. 90 Young maiden's apron, *pepetu,* Ndebele. KwaNdebele, South Africa. December 1980.

Fig. 91 Layers of brass rings considered a sign of beauty, wealth, and self-respect, Ndebele. Kwa-Ndebele, South Africa. December 1980.

115

beaded calabashes with water, pour this over the father, and dance. This custom indicates that the father will ultimately receive bride-price, *lobolo*. A baby boy is dressed in a beaded loincloth made of leather, *lebeshu*, and two strings of white and red beads, *dikhoso*. At four months, the girl wears a *ghabi*, a beaded loincloth made by the maternal grandmother. This frontal skirt is about 10 centimetres square and has a border of beads at the top from which hang strands of twisted sisal trimmed with beads. (Fig. 88) This type of dress is worn until the girl is about twelve years old.

At three months of age, the baby is 'taken out', *uphelaphandle*, for the first time, for everyone in the community to see. A party and dancing celebration ensue. At this time, the mother wears a *mapoto*, as well as a beaded blanket, *umakhomo*. She covers her face with red paste, *letsuku*, a commercially prepared mixture which she wears until she stops breast-feeding. Some of the women wear the *mapoto* daily while others have changed from this traditional dress to a *khiba*, made from commercial brown cloth with white spots. Recently, this attire has become the 'traditional' dress, replacing the *mapoto* and the back apron, *isithimba*, which were worn on a daily basis.

When youngsters approach puberty, further delineation of their situation is made manifest by the characteristics of the appropriate bead-work. A white flag outside the hut indicates to the community that the son of the house is attending the initiation or mountain school. The boy, aged about sixteen, spends three to six months at the school and, during that time, the mother mourns for him. Her token of mourning is expressed by growing her hair (the Ndebele women follow a custom of shaving their hair as they believe that long hair indicates stupidity[77]), and by wearing long strips of bead-work, *siyaya*. These side veils symbolize tears because her son will now progress from boyhood to manhood. (Fig. 89) When the boy returns from the school, he wears a Cleopatra-type beaded headpiece with beaded band which frames the face, *tomo*, as well as a beaded skin-blanket, *lenaka*. On this rare occasion, the father, too, wears traditional dress, that of a V-shaped leather apron which stretches from neck to lower abdomen. The father holds a leather shield while the mother carries the *tondrola*, a long, beaded stick, in the left hand and a short beaded stick in the right hand. When the initiate arrives home, a new name is bestowed upon him which is only used by the parents.

During puberty, the young female also attends initiation school. At that time, she wears a skirt made of unravelled hopsacking. The skirt, *titana*, is beaded around the border, although the skirt remains unbeaded when a girl is not a virgin. During the initiation ceremony itself, the initiate wears six hoops of beads around her waist. These hoops, *nkolawane*, mimic the elongated figures of fertility dolls. One week after the initiation, some of the hoops are removed and passed on to other initiates. The dress at this time also includes a leather covering on the buttock, *sithimba*, and, if she is engaged, includes a black beaded belt, *isiko*. The puberty rites end with the graduate wearing a new beaded garment, the rectangular *pepetu*, or maiden's apron, indicating that the young woman is now available for marriage. (Fig. 90)

Beaded hoops, which women wear from youth through their married lives, are also significant, and they are removed only upon the death of a husband. As is the case with the apron styling, different types of beaded hoops indicate

116

different stages in a woman's life. Around the neck, arms, and legs, young girls wear hoops constructed by coiling bundles of dried grass or corn leaves and tying them together with cotton to form circles. These hoops are heavily encrusted with strands of unicoloured beads, which are often built directly on the girl's body. Occasionally, metal drawing-pins purchased at the local store provide additional decoration to these solid hoops. Women about to be married often have a witch-doctor fit and solder layers of brass rings around their necks and legs. (Fig.91) These rings, *izixolwana*, are considered a sign of beauty, wealth, and self-respect among the Ndebele.

Bead-work plays a role in the courtship rites of the young Ndebele, as well. If a woman receives a beaded tab or love-letter and wears it instead of dropping it to the ground, she indicates that she loves the sender. He then wears a headband with two beaded flaps, *sikiliti,* to cover his ears, which symbolically prevents him from hearing other females. This is one of the few times in which men wear beaded adornments because, for the most part, their dress is Western.

As might be expected, the bead-work associated with marriage and the marital ritual is more complex and diverse. When an Ndebele couple decide to get married, a series of formalized negotiations begin among the respective parents. To the parents of each wife he marries, a man must give *lobolo*, or bride-price, of six head of cattle. Then, three months before the wedding, the bride's father is free to kill a sheep and work the skin until it takes the shape of a wrap. The bride-to-be and friends then work on the bead-work design, add a heavy beaded shawl across the shoulders, and create a bead-work border. Thus is produced one of a woman's most cherished possessions, her bridal cloak. She might even consider wearing it again, sometime in the future, when her son goes to initiation school.

On the wedding-day, the young woman reveals her changed status by changing her *pepetu* for a new apron, the wedding apron, *jocolo*, which she will wear until she bears a child, at which time her transition from adolescent to mother/artisan will be complete and she will remove the *jocolo* to replace it, finally, with the symbol of motherhood, the beaded *mapoto*. The *jocolo*, whose five panels are said to symbolize the deposit of five head of cattle toward the bride-price, *lobolo*, is made by the paternal grandmother. (Fig. 92) The groom's family pays for the bride and her dress. Occasionally, there is an additional miniature panel on either side of the five panels. This touch signifies that the wearer is not the groom's first wife. (Fig. 92, example on right)

White beads predominate in the complete bridal costume. (Fig. 93) The bride emerges virtually hidden from view and is weighted down by the elaborate attire. The long, beaded wedding veil, *nyoga*, is a snake-like train which hangs from the shoulders and trails on the ground, creating a wave-like motion as the bride walks and dances. Like the *jocolo*, often as long as 1,5 metres and approximately 20 to 40 centimetres wide, the *nyoga* is made by the paternal grandmother, as well. Square holes across its width means the bride is not the first wife,[78] while a flap woven at the end of the train indicates that the bride is a virgin. If the patterns are divided into 3 to 5 sections down the length of the train, the bride is notified that her husband intends to take more than one wife, and by wearing the train, she agrees to his inten-

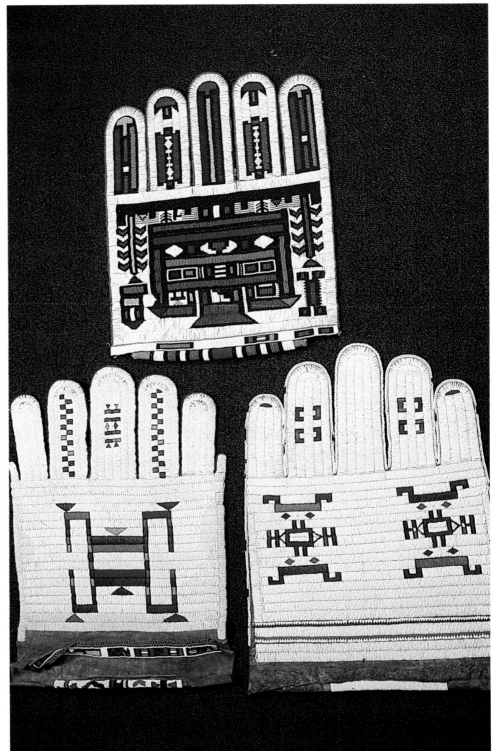

Fig. 92 Five-panelled *jo-colo* worn on wedding-day, Ndebele. *Author's collection.*

Opposite page: Fig. 93 Complete bridal costume, Ndebele, KwaNdebele, South Africa. December 1980.

tion. Designs vary as the older examples seem to be predominantly white and less patterned than those of more recent creations. Westernization's effects are evident in newer designs which are geometric, often three-dimensional in effect, and include triangles, rectangles, parallelograms, diamonds, arcs, and wavy lines, and they may include alphabetic lettering which the people absorb from vehicle number-plates or architectural studies.

In addition to the heavily beaded train, the bride wears the following: a white beaded headband about 2,5 centimetres wide, *umgaka*; a beaded front wedding veil, *siyaya*, to cover her face (Fig. 93); a wedding blanket, *orare*, which has been beaded by the bride's sisters; and the prized bridal cloak. In her hand she carries a beaded bridal stick with a wooden head, although in recent years a tennis-ball often replaces the wooden head.

Once the young married woman has borne a child, her status as a parent is revealed by changing her *jocolo* for a *mapoto* (Fig. 94), an apron of goat-skin or canvas base which is beaded using the lazy-stitch sewing typical of this kind of Ndebele work. The *mapoto* is distinguished by its size, texture, and shape. It is rectangular, having two flaps on either side of the base. With beaded tassels between the flaps, decoration varies, although it appears that modern *mapoto* are more colourfully beaded than those made before the 1970s. This difference is true of Ndebele bead-work in general; older work is marked by a predominance of white in the background, more subdued col-ouration, and subtle linear designs of greater intricacy, in contrast to designs of more recent origin as previously noted. Ndebele belts are now popular with tourists and newer harsh colouring and simplified tracery characterize these articles made for trade.

Once married, the importance of fertility is no less a part of the Ndebele's concern, and the existence of beaded fertility dolls, *umtwana wa madlozi*, suggests this significance in the life of the Ndebele woman (Fig. 95) At initia-tion school the young girl receives her own doll which she will cherish until her first pregnancy. Custom has it that, after the birth of the third child, the fertility doll must be given away, sold, or destroyed because it is considered unlucky to keep the doll any longer. The doll, in addition to symbolizing fer-tility, also symbolizes the desire for a woman to have a beautiful baby.

In addition to being fertility symbols, beaded dolls play a role in court-ship. In this instance, 'selector dolls' are placed outside the home of a pro-spective bride. By placing a doll outside the woman's house, the suitor indi-cates his intention to make a proposal. When a chief wishes to take another bride, he places three dolls on an eating mat, each one symbolizing a wife. The number of dolls sitting on the mat signifies the number of wives he in-tends to have. Symbolically, beaded dolls assist in establishing the bride-price between father and groom. If the bride-to-be is not a virgin, the groom places an armless doll before the father indicating that he intends to pay a lower price than requested. On the day that the bride-price is paid, the mater-nal grandmother secretly makes a doll for the future bride. No one may enter the hut during the time she is fashioning the image, and after the wedding ceremony, when the bride enters her new hut, the grandmother ritually pre-sents her with the new doll which must be kept in the dark in a corner of the hut. At the same time, another doll is placed between the couple and if the

120

wife fails to conceive, the maternal grandmother makes still another doll for them.

Beaded dolls vary in size and shape. Old beads from a used *pepetu* are incorporated into the hoops encircling the body of the doll. The body is constructed from tightly wrapped old rags and then covered with a layer of beads over which predominantly white beaded hoops are placed, although splashes of blue, red, green, and orange are also used. The faces are usually pink, while the hair is consistently black. An unusual male/female pair of dolls that was found in the field belonged to an old Ndebele royal family. (Fig. 95, right) The male doll, named 'Mkonyen Masombuka', sports a Western hat and tie. The female, 'Nandali Mahlongu', wears a beaded head-dress reminiscent of the bridal garb.

The symbolism of the *sangoma* or witch-doctor's attire can, thus, be readily understood. (Fig. 96) Worn over the *umatjeka*, a beaded, pleated skirt fashioned of red cloth with white beads, and the *isiquata*, a small apron-canvas with beads, is the *isorika*, a black/red caftan top trimmed with white beads. Urban contact has altered these connotations, however, as gradual change has caused shifts in meaning which render interpretation difficult.

The last cycle marked by Ndebele ceremonial bead-work is death. When widowed, the Ndebele woman sheds her beads at her husband's funeral and wears a beadless skin with a dark blanket. After a year of mourning, she may adorn herself with some of her prized possessions. Traditionally, when a female died, her beads were buried with her, although today these are either passed down in the family or sold. Increasingly, the economic difficulties faced by the Ndebele force the women to sell rare, precious artefacts like initiation, pre-initiation, and married women's aprons, belts, and fertility dolls used in traditional rituals and never before readily available to the market-place. Garments that were passed down from generation to generation as treasured possessions or dowries are now dispersed, threatening a valuable cultural heritage.

Just as ceremonial bead-work marks female maturational stages and marital status, so does the Ndebele house decoration follow the female's passage from girlhood to womanhood, in addition to mirroring the annual environmental cycle. It is at puberty, during a girl's seclusion period, that she learns the art of elaborate mural decoration as part of her preparation for the coming-out festival in which she and her peers will participate.[79] In this polygamous society, each wife has her own hut, built and decorated according to ancient custom. Before a hut is constructed, a traditional ritual of 'doctoring' the foundation takes place. Pegs are smeared with medicinal ointment and buried at the corners and centre of the site to protect the inhabitants from evil spirits coming within the boundaries marked by the pegs.[80] After the summer rains have washed away the elaborately decorated paintwork, the women of the village resurface the house walls with cow dung and mud and then proceed to redecorate. Decorations vary from year to year, as shown by Figures 97 and 98, both photographed at the same site, one year apart.

These house decorations, which are refurbished annually, demonstrate the spontaneity of the artisans, and the aesthetic vitality and the preference for symmetry that also characterize the Ndebele bead-work. The artisan's lack of

Fig. 94 Married woman's apron, *mapoto*, Ndebele. KwaNdebele, South Africa. December 1980.

Opposite page: above, Fig. 95 Ndebele fertility dolls, *umtwana wa madlozi*, Ndebele. *Author's collection; below,* Fig. 97 Painted façade, 1980, Ndebele. KwaNdebele, South Africa. December 1980.

122

Fig. 96 Female witch-doctor in traditional garb, Ndebele. KwaNdebele, South Africa. December 1976.

preliminary design or planning work is evident in their house decoration as they begin their murals with free-hand painting of whitewash outlines to form the basic motifs. (Fig. 99) Sometimes these outlines encompass an entire wall's dimensions. Similarly, bead-work patterns are worked out directly on the garment or ornament, with no preliminary drawing.

The use of brilliant colours in decorative Ndebele artwork reveals their aesthetic liveliness and suggests a flamboyance especially characteristic of

124

the mural art. In house decoration, brightly coloured commercial paints, featuring blues, greens, reds, browns, yellows, and whites, have replaced the traditional natural soot, ash, and clay ochres obtained from the earth. (Fig. 100) Likewise, the maiden's beaded apron is characterized by its bright colour, although the married woman's apron is distinguished from its predecessor by the fact that more recent examples are less predominantly white, featuring more colour.

The Ndebele preference for symmetry is shown in their crafts, as well. In house decoration, the outlines are filled in with elaborate and bold, balanced patterns. The geometric motifs, which are repeated in different combinations produce a striking variety of decoration, including squares, rectangles, circles, spheres, and triangles. The women's preference for balanced motifs and gabled walls is revealed in their architectural designs and is one of several geometric designs which often appears on the married woman's beaded apron. Interspersed with these forms are images of a wider variety, including popular alphabet and number motifs, car registration numbers, and silhouetted flowers, birds, animals, and snakes. This profusion of man-made symbols is notable when viewed from the perspective that it is the women who are the artists and it is they who are limited to a rural existence. Three-dimensional architectural motifs are to be found as well as exotic abstractions, but there is infrequent use of human figures.

While the characteristics of Ndebele bead-work and house decoration reflect the noted similarities, alterations in both art-forms are evolving at increasingly rapid rates. As Westernization encroaches on the Ndebele, changes are occurring that make ceremonial bead-work and house decoration endangered art-forms. New paints and new images are being added to the Ndebele artisan's repertoire at the same time that some villagers are no longer decorating their homes. It has become either too expensive or there is a declining concern among a younger generation not interested in preserving their culture. At the same time, the construction of the homes themselves increasingly reflects the effects of modernization as thatch roofs are replaced with corrugated metal, and an unembellished façade indicates proximity to town as it denotes class advancement. (Fig. 101) Contemporary images of urban derivation such as aeroplane motifs, alphabet lettering, and telephone poles are a few of the motifs that continue to dilute traditional symbols. Brightly coloured and plastic beads are replacing the purity of the white and glass beads of yesterday. *Mapoto* made from plastic sheets and plastic beads are replacing the traditional goat-skin and glass-beaded aprons. Both bead-work and mural art are in transitional stages as the exigencies of drought, poor soil, poverty, and economics have tended to override the demands of tradition and the pursuit of these art-forms. Ndebele means 'fugitive' or 'refugee', and as traditions are threatened and lost, the Ndebele artisan and his art face a future as tenuous as that of the refugee for whom his people have been named.

Following pages: above left, Fig. 98 Same wall as Fig. 97, painted in 1981. December 1981; *below left,* Fig. 99 Murals painted free-hand by women, Ndebele. KwaNdebele, South Africa. December 1975; *above right,* Fig. 100 Bold, geometric house decoration using commercial paints, Ndebele. KwaNdebele, South Africa, December 1980; *below right,* Fig. 101 Modern tin-roofed, unembellished home, Ndebele. Marble Hall, KwaNdebele, South Africa. December 1980.

6 Conclusions

The art of any culture should be viewed in such a way that its context is respected, certainly not an unusual requirement, yet one that with respect to the arts of the African tradition has frequently been paid lip-service, if not ignored. In a peculiar paradox however, today, in the case of the art we have considered in this book, the cultural context reflects a dual influence—that of tradition and acculturation existing side by side, affecting one another in a constant interplay. It is intriguing if not exciting, but would be more so if it were not for the fact that a cultural tradition is now endangered, its very existence threatened where not already extinct. In point of fact, moreover, we have seen but a representative sampling of the material traditions of southern Africa, those chosen for their distinctiveness and which must be recorded before they fade into African artistic and cultural history. One is struck by the enormity of such a task and its attendant implications but encouraged, nonetheless, by the urgency that accompanies it.

It is important to note that, as early as the fifteenth century, Western historians record an indigenous African artistic response to the effects of European exploration, while in southern Africa, the artistic outgrowths of the effects of explorers, traders, hunters, and missionaries, especially, have been recorded only since the early nineteenth century.

It was the church's influence more than any other that brought Christianity and education to the African 'heathen'. The profound impact of this development cannot be emphasized enough. With the individual's shift in allegiance to God came the breakdown of loyalty to the clan, and a threat to everything this meant, including ancestor worship, traditional religion, and attendant ceremonies like those to ensure the land's fertility and rituals marking life's milestones.[81]

Westernization introduced the notion of the money economy and taxation soon followed, harming the kinship system which heretofore had provided for all material needs through elaborate delineations of responsibility among one's kin.[82] These factors led to cultural changes that were, as we have seen, increasingly reflected in the material cultures of the native Africans who, often from economic necessity, were forced into a face-to-face exposure to Western values and artefacts. At the same time, Christian missionaries deliberately sabotaged or destroyed those articles considered heathen, and the converted themselves began to eschew the traditional. Mission schools, in turn, frequently taught the people to look down upon an 'in-

Opposite page: Fig. 102 Traditional fertility doll incorporating modern materials, Ndebele. *Author's collection.*

ferior' cultural heritage, as the benefits of education and resulting value shifts linked modern material possessions to new notions of wealth and status. Taught to dislike and devalue their own, the process of incorporating the Western began as plastic replaced fibre and grass, manufactured cloth supplanted hide, tin or aluminium replaced thatch, commercial paints substituted for ochres, and Western motifs, artefacts, and symbols found their way into southern African tribal expression.

As already noted, however, Western market influences have, for the present, staved off the extinction of some tribal art-forms, although this salutary development is tempered by the changed and changing character of the material culture, subject, as it is, to the aesthetic requirements and limitations of the Western market. And yet, the old ways struggle to exist as the traditional is slowly altered in an amalgam of old and new. Martin West and Jean Morris in their book, *Abantu*, have summarized this development.

Examples of this abound; the ancestors, for example, may now be incorporated into Christian beliefs and have taken on something of the status of saints; a diviner may be a practising Christian with some knowledge of Western medicine. Today, the bride-wealth is often paid in cash and a couple may choose to be married by both traditional and civil rites. School holidays dictate the timing of initiation and some boys are sent to hospitals to be circumcised in clinical surroundings. In fact, even when things do not appear to have changed, the *attitudes* of people towards them may well be different.[83]

But some attitudes remain the same and one that continues to pervade indigenous tribal value systems is their belief in frugality, expressed in the re-use of any article available, whether a throwaway or those chosen for purposeful recycling or updating. Upon their return from the big city, their work in the mines, or from their travels, the tribal people bring with them their found objects, discards of no value to most, articles like bottle caps, soft drink container tabs, used plastic bags, empty glass bottles, and miscellaneous buttons. To these they may add their new acquisitions from the towns — tin and enamel household utensils, glass bottles, plastic pails and containers, tin foil and paper wrappings, tin cans, striped cable wire, and aluminium siding, to list but a few. Incorporating these items into their traditional art-forms, the Zulu, Basotho, Bayei, Hambukushu, Herero, and Ndebele produce a transitional art, the evidence of which is a striking display of objects.

Figure 102 is an Ndebele doll, a *tour de force* of ingenious blending of traditional doll styling with found objects. Manufactured woven wool covers the head which is adorned with a soda-pop pull tab and which, when grouped and strung, form a belt to decorate the waist. Zippers make up the arms and form the necklace which covers the woven orange bag seam, both adorning the neck. Finally, a discarded plastic garbage bag skirts this intriguing figure who yet retains her traditional character.

Possessing a visual affinity to her is the Zulu fertility doll of Figure 103. Large plastic beads supplement the traditional glass that predominates on the figure, while brass studs and a necklace of recent design adorn this doll that continues to reflect traditional Zulu colour preferences and motifs.

As we have seen, useful garments mirror acculturation, this condition revealed by the necklace in Figure 104. Discarded glass ampules from a medical

Opposite page: Fig. 103 Traditional fertility doll incorporating modern materials, Zulu. *Author's collection.*

131

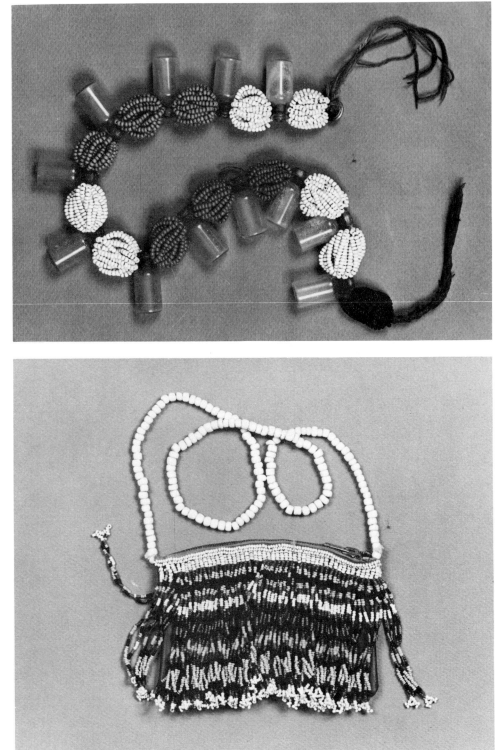

Fig.104 Traditional beaded necklace incorporating discarded glass bottles, Zulu. *Author's collection.*

Fig.105 Zippered plastic purse covered with traditional bead-work, Zulu. *Author's collection.*

132

Fig. 106 Telephone-cable wire in traditional design covering a modern glass milk bottle, Zulu. *Author's collection.*

clinic are secured to this beaded necklace by threading twine about their grooved, recessed necks, although, once again, the traditional beaded construction and patterning remain. Over a small, plastic purse in Figure 105, an overlay of fringed beads in characteristic Zulu design has been attached while the handle is constructed of the modern plastic beads we encountered earlier. Finally, mass communication has made inroads in southern African tribal consciousness as revealed by Figure 106. Multicoloured strands of telephone-cable wire have created a finely woven covering for a glass milk bottle — another implement of modern manufacture. The zigzag design, however, retains aspects of traditional Zulu bead-work.

As noted earlier, semi-permanence must be a fact of life among many tribal people of southern Africa and, among the Bayei and Hambukushu, it is required by the cattle grazing which is the economic mainstay of their culture. It is not surprising, then, that the Hambukushu have designed dwellings that appear semi-permanent to the Western eye, in any case. A home encountered on the road to Gomare features walls and foundations of sand-filled discarded beer cans. Nor, is it unusual to encounter a basket whose design graphically displays the results of their continual interaction with Western culture. (Fig. 107)

133

Fig.108 Chief wearing traditional blanket over modern clothing and standing in front of contemporary building, Basotho. Roma, kingdom of Lesotho, southern Africa. December 1975.

At the same time, however, we have seen that modern dwellings are highly prized among the tribal peoples and among them, it is the Basotho who, in the greatest numbers, have replaced the hut, as well as their traditional attire. In Figure 108, the Basotho chief of Saint Michaels stands before a modern, whitewashed, cinder-block dwelling featuring manufactured hardware and window panes, draped in the 'Badges of the Bear' blanket covering Western style trousers and modern shoes. In contrast, in Figure 109 we see a Herero woman attired in modern dress of commercially produced fabric, sporting a commercially woven headband below her old-style hat and carrying a Herero doll that features the bygone traditional costume of the Herero woman.

This visual display of acculturation attests dramatically to the effects of Westernization on the tribal peoples of southern Africa. Their cultural and value traditions in flux, they incorporate this dynamic within their artistic expression, creating a visual panoply intriguing in its history at the same time that its evolution endangers the traditions themselves. While it is, perhaps, inevitable that some will be irretrievably lost or altered, we may hope that increased interest and awareness among the people themselves and outsiders will save them before endangerment becomes extinction and museums protect all that remains of a rich artistic tradition.

Opposite page: Fig. 107 Basket incorporating English-language letters and numbers, Bayei. *Author's collection.*

135

Fig.109 Old-style hat, modern dress, and traditional doll utilizing contemporary fabric and notions of colour and design, Herero. Etsha village, Ngamiland, Botswana. July 1982. *Courtesy of Peter Nelson.*

136

Notes

1 Nelson H.H. Graburn, *Ethnic and Tourist Arts*, (Berkeley: University of California Press, 1976), p. 12.

2 Ibid., p. 26.

3 Ibid., p. 15

4 Ibid., p. 26.

5 Martin West, Jean Morris, *Abantu*, (Cape Town: C. Struik, 1976), p. 37.

6 Ibid., p. 38.

7 Ibid., p. 38.

8 Ibid., p. 38.

9 Rhoda Levinsohn, 'Rural KwaZulu Basketry', *African Arts*, vol. 14, no. 1. (Nov. 1980), p. 52.

10 Hugh Ashton, *The Basotho*, (London: Oxford University Press, 1967), p. 10.

11 David Ambrose, *The Guide to Lesotho*, (Johannesburg: Winchester Press, 1974), p. 19.

12 Ashton, *The Basotho*, p. 21.

13 James Walton, 'South African Peasant Architecture', *African Studies*, vol. 7, no. 4 (Dec. 1948), p. 141.

14 G.E. Nettleton, 'History of the Ngamiland Tribes up to 1926', *Bantu Studies*, vol. 8, no. 4, (Dec. 1934), p. 355.

15 Ibid.

16 T. Thou, 'The Taming of the Okavango Swamps—the Utilization of a Riverine Environment 1750–1800', *Botswana Notes and Records*, (Gaborone: The Botswana Society), p. 152.

17 Author's conversation with the resettlement officer of Etsha, Malcolm Thomas, August 1977.

18 Thou, *Botswana Notes and Records*, vol. 4, p. 152.

19 Evert Voorthuizen, 'Thatching in Botswana', *Botswana Notes and Records*, vol. 8, (Gaborone: The Botswana Society, 1976), p. 169.

20 Frank Vivelo, *The Herero of Western Botswana: Aspects of Change in a group of Bantu-speaking Cattle Herders,* (New Jersey: Rutgers University, 1974), p. 3.

21 Gordon Gibson, 'Double Descent and Its Correlates among the Herero of Ngamiland', *American Anthropologist*, vol. 58, no. 1, (Feb. 1956), p. 112.

22 Ibid., p. 113.

23 Voorthuizen, *Thatching in Botswana*, p. 169.

24 Hendrik Luttig, *Religious System and Social Organization of the Herero*, (Utrecht: Kemink en Zoon, 1933), p. 3.

25 Ashton, *The Basotho*, p. 93.

26 Barbara Tyrell, *Suspicion is my Name*, (Cape Town: Gothic Printing Co., 1971), p. 83.

27 I. Schapera, *The Tswana*, (London: London International African Institute: Ethnographic Survey of Africa, part 3), p. 21.

28 E.K. Afriyie, 'Human Resources of the Okavango area: Some Implications for Development Projects', *Okavango Delta Symposium*, (Gaborone: Gaborone Press, 1976), p. 179.

29 Author's conversation with Gaylard Kombani, guide and interpreter, Ngamiland, August 1977.

30 Author's conversation with Bayei weaver, Kejemg Matenge, village of Gomare, Ngamiland, August 1977.

31 Author's conversation with Gaylard Kombani.

32 Author's conversation with weaver, Ikeletseng Makondo, Gomare village, Ngamiland, August 1977.

33 Ashton, *The Basotho*, p. 129.

34 Ibid.

35 Graburn, *Ethnic and Tourist Arts*, p. 2.

36 Graburn, op. cit., 'Commercial fine arts or pseudo-traditional arts—although they are made with eventual sale in mind, they adhere to culturally embedded aesthetic and formal standards', p. 6.

37 Graburn, *Ethnic and Tourist Arts*, p. 14.

38 Author's conversation with Reverend Lofroth, co-ordinator and promoter of Zulu handicraft, KwaZulu, February 1978.

39 Author's conversation with Reverend Lofroth, co-ordinator and promoter of Zulu handicraft, KwaZulu, February 1978.

40 Author's conversation with Michael Yoffe, Botswana, August 1977.

41 Quality is determined by technical proficiency, i.e. baskets should be sturdy, lids should fit properly, and shape should be balanced and not lopsided. Quality, of course varies, and where possible, inferior baskets are not purchased. Author's conversation with Michael Yoffe.

42 Graburn, *Ethnic and Tourist Arts,* p. 295.

43 Justinus Sechefo, *The Old Clothing of the Basotho*, (Basutoland: The Catholic Centre), p. 23.

44 Thomas Larson, 'Craftwork of the Hambukushu of Botswana', Botswana Notes and Records, vol. 7, (Gaborone: The Botswana Society, 1975), p. 111.

45 Rhoda Levinsohn, 'Symbolic Significance of Traditional Zulu Beadwork', *Black Art*, vol. 3, no. 4, 1979, pp. 29—35.

46 Rhoda Levinsohn, 'Rural KwaZulu Basketry', *African Arts,* Nov. 1980, pp. 52—7.

47 J.W. Grossert, *Zulu Crafts*, (Pietermaritzburg: Shuter and Shooter, 1978), p. 33.

48 A.T. Bryant, *The Zulu People*, (Pietermaritzburg: Shuter and Shooter, 1949), p. 275.

49 Hilgard Schoeman, *The Zulu*, (Cape Town: Purnell, 1975), n.p.

50 Information obtained from interpreters and guides Tulani Zulu and Ambrose Ngvbese, KwaZulu, August 1981.

51 Barbara Tyrell, *Suspicion is my Name*, p. 83.

52 Rhoda Levinsohn, 'Rural KwaZulu Basketry', *African Arts*, vol. 14, no. 1, Nov. 1980, p. 57.

53 Hilgard Schoeman, 'Beadwork in the Cultural Tradition of the Zulu 1', *Lantern*, Sept. 1971, p. 41.

54 Walter Battiss, *The Art of Africa*, (Pietermaritzburg: Shuter and Shooter, 1958), p. 137.

55 Robin St. John, 'The Bead Love Letters of Zululand'. Information obtained from the Africana Museum, Johannesburg, South Africa.

56 'The Beadwork of South Africa', 12—31 March 1962, City of Johannesburg, Africana Museum, p. 2.

57 Walter Battiss, *The Art of Africa*, p. 135.

58 Hilgard Schoeman, 'Beadwork in the Cultural Tradition of the Zulu 1', p. 42.

59 Regina G. Twala, 'Beads as Regulating the Social Life of the Zulu and Swazi', *African Studies*, 10, (1951), pp. 113—23.

60 Green, *umanlambo*, most often means sickness, particularly lovesickness or a fainting feeling, or discord, although green may also signify contentment or domestic joy. Pink beads, *imfinginga*, usually mean poverty and sometimes laziness, although they also stand for high rank or an oath. Yellow beads of pumpkin or calf excrement, *iphuzi* or

utuvi benkonyame, respectively, most often stand for wealth, particularly cattle which are used to pay the bride-price, *lobola*, but can also represent a garden or domestic diligence in addition to carrying the negative connotations of thirst, withering away, or evil. Blues and greys, which are sometimes used interchangeably with blues, have several distinct hues, each with its set of meanings, while often bead colours have opaque as well as transparent forms, each having a different name as well as significance. For example, opaque red, *umgazi*, signifies blood, while transparent red, *umlilwana*, means fire. Either can be used to convey a message of strong emotion, a 'burning heart', anger, or the redness of eyes from continually seeking one's lover in vain.

61 'Hair Styles and Trimmings', *Bantu*, vol. 13, no. 7 (1966), p. 202.

62 Eileen Jensen Krige, *The Social System of the Zulus*, (London: Longmans, Green and Co., 1936), p. 372.

63 Barbara Tyrell, *Tribal Peoples of Southern Africa*, (Cape Town: T.V. Bulpin, 1968), p. 122.

64 Ibid, p. 100.

65 François Laydevant, *The Basuto*, (Lesotho: The Social Studies Centre), p. 63.

66 James Walton, *Father of Kindness and Father of Horses*, (Lesotho: Morija Printing Works), p. 41.

67 Information obtained from manager of a local blanket factory, Johannesburg, February 1979).

68 Thomas Larson, 'Craftwork of the Hambukushu of Botswana', p. 118.

69 Ibid.

70 Barbara Tyrell, *Tribal Peoples of Southern Africa*, p. 14.

71 *Natural History,* vol. 3, (March 1969), p. 48.

72 Ibid., P. 50.

73 E.H.L. Schwartz, *The Kalahari and its Native Races*, (London: H.F.G. Witherby, 1928), p. 213.

74 H.L. Hahn, H. Vedder, *The Native Tribes of South West Africa*, (Frank Cass and Co., Ltd., 1966), p. 182.

75 Ibid.

76 Peter Becker, *Inland Tribes of Southern Africa*, (Granada Publishing, 1979), p. 59.

77 Information obtained from guides and interpreters in the field.

78 Information obtained from guides and interpreters in the field.

79 Barbara Tyrell, *Tribal Peoples of Southern Africa*, p. 83.

80 I. Schapera, 'The Ndebele of South Africa', *Natural History*, 58, (1949), p. 410.

81 D.H. Reader, *Zulu Tribes in Transition*, (Manchester: Manchester University Press, 1966), p. 338.

82 West and Morris, *Abantu*, p. 169.

83 Ibid., p. 170.

141

Select Bibliography

Afriyie, E.K. 'Human Resources of the Okavango area: Some Implications for Development Projects', *Okavango Delta Symposium*, Botswana: The Botswana Society, 1976, pp. 179–86.

Alberti, L. *De Kaffers aan de Zuidkust van Afrika.* Amsterdam: Maaskamp, 1810.

Ambrose, D. *The Guide to Lesotho.* Johannesburg: Winchester Press, 1974.

Andersson, C.J. *Lake Ngami.* Cape Town: C. Struik, 1967.

Ashton, Hugh. *The Basuto.* London: Oxford University Press, 1952.

Axel, Ivar. *Zulu Thought-Patterns and Symbolism.* London: C. Hurst and Co., 1976.

Battiss, Walter. *The Art of Africa.* Pietermaritzburg: Shuter and Shooter, 1958.

Becker, P. *Inland Tribes of Southern Africa.* Granada Publishing, 1979.

Becker, Peter. *Trails and Tribes in Southern Africa.* London: Hart-Davis, MacGibbon, 1975.

————; Laubser, W.; and Strydom, F. *Die Volkere van Suid-Afrika.* Johannesburg: Dagbreek Boekhandel, 1960.

Bronttem, B., and Lang, A. 'Zulu Beadwork', *African Arts*, vol. 6, no. 3, 1973, pp. 8–13 and p. 64.

Brown, T. *Among the Zulu Nomads.* London: 1926.

Bruwer, P., and Van Schalkwyk, J.P. *Die Bantoe van Suid-Afrika.* Johannesburg: Afrikaanse Pers-boekhandel, 1957.

Bryant, A.T. *History of the Zulus.* Cape Town: C. Struik, 1964.

————. *The Zulu People.* Pietermaritzburg: Shuter and Shooter, 1949.

Campbell, A.C. 'Traditional Utilization of the Okavango Delta', *Okavango Delta Symposium*, Botswana: The Botswana Society, 1976, pp. 163–74.

Casalis, J.E. *The Basuto.* London: Nisbet, 1861.

Coertze, P.J. 'Huweliksgewoontes en erfreg by die Batlokwa van Basotoeland', *Bantu Studies*, vol. 7, 1931, pp. 257–73.

Eloff, J. *Etnografiese Studies in Suidelike-Afrika*. Pretoria: J.L. van Schaik, 1972.

Frank, Oswald. *Aankoms van die Bantoes in Suid-Afrika*. Pretoria: Noordelike Drukpers, 1931.

Gibson, G. 'Double Descent and its Correlates among the Herero of Ngamiland', *American Anthropologist*, vol. 58, no. 1. February 1956.

Graburn, Nelson H.H. *Ethnic and Tourist Arts*. Los Angeles: University of California Press, 1976.

Grossert, J.W. *Zulu Crafts*. Pietermaritzburg: Shuter and Shooter, 1978.

Grossert, John W. *Arts and Crafts for Africans*. Pietermaritzburg: Shuter and Shooter, 1953.

Hahn, H.L., and Vedder, H. *The Native Tribes of South West Africa*. London: Frank Cass and Co., Ltd., 1966.

Hudson, E. *Volkekundige Studies*. Cape Town: Nasionale Boekhandel, 1958.

Jackson, Agnes. *'n Besoek aan Zoeloeland*. Cape Town: Oxford University Press, 1960.

Jopling, Carol F. *Art and Aesthetics in Primitive Societies*. New York: E.P. Dutton and Co. Inc., 1971.

Krige, E.J. *The Social System of the Zulus*. London: Longmans, Green and Co., 1936.

Lambrecht, Dora. 'Basketry in Ngamiland', *Botswana Notes and Records*, vol. 8, Gaborone: The Botswana Society, 1976, pp. 179—88.

Larson, Thomas. 'The Hambukushu of Ngamiland', *Botswana Notes and Records*, vol. 2, Gaborone: The Botswana Society, 1970, pp. 29—43.

————. 'Craftwork of the Hambukushu of Botswana', *Botswana Notes and Records*, vol. 7, Gaborone: The Botswana Society, 1975, pp. 109—20.

Lawton, A.C. 'Bantu Pottery of Southern Africa', *Annals of the South African Museum*, vol. 49, Part 1, September 1967.

Laydevant, F. *The Basuto*. Lesotho: The Social Studies Centre.

Levinsohn, Rhoda. 'Symbolic Significance of Traditional Zulu Beadwork', *Black Art*, vol. 3, no. 4, 1979, pp. 29—35.

————. 'Symbolic Design in Bayei Basketry', *Black Art*, vol. 3, no. 2, 1979, pp. 56—63.

————. 'Ndebele Beadwork', *Ornament*, vol. 4, no. 2, August 1979, pp. 61—3.

————. *Basketry: A Renaissance in Southern Africa*. Cleveland: Protea Press, 1979.

————. 'Rural KwaZulu Basketry', *African Arts*, vol. 14, no. 1. November 1980, p. 52.

Luttig, H. *Religious System and Social Organization of the Herero*. Utrecht: Kemink en Zoon, 1933.

Meyerowitz, H.V. *A Report on the Possibility of the Development of Village Crafts in Basutoland*. Basutoland: Morija Printing Works, 1936.

Nettleton, G.E. 'History of the Ngamiland Tribes up to 1926', *Bantu Studies*, vol. 9, no. 4, December 1934, p. 355.

Reader, D.H. *Zulu Tribes in Transition*. Manchester: Manchester University Press, 1966.

Schapera, I. 'The Ndebele of South Africa', *Natural History*, 58, 1949, p. 410.

————. *The Ethnic Composition of Tswana Tribes*. London: Lund Humphries, 1952.

————. 'The Tswana', *Ethnographic Survey of Africa*, Part 3, London: International African Institute, 1953.

Schoeman H. 'Beadwork in the Cultural Tradition of the Zulu', *Lantern*, September 1971, pp. 37—42.

————. *The Zulu*. Cape Town: Purnell, 1975.

Schwartz, E.H.L. *The Kalahari and its Native Races*. London: H.F.G. Witherby, 1928.

Sechefo, J. *The Old Clothing of the Basotho*. Basutoland: The Catholic Centre, no date.

Thou, T. 'The Taming of the Okavango Swamps—the Utilization of a Riverine Environment 1750—1800', *Botswana Notes and Records*. Gaborone: The Botswana Society, p. 152.

Twala, R. 'Beads as Regulating the Social Life of the Zulu and Swazi', *African Studies*, vol. 10, 1951, pp. 113—23.

Tyrell, B. *Suspicion is my Name*. Cape Town: Gothic Printing Co., 1971.

————. *Tribal Peoples of Southern Africa*. Cape Town: T.V. Bulpin, 1968.

Vivelo, F. *The Herero of Western Botswana: Aspects of Change in a Group of Bantu-speaking Cattle Herders*. New Jersey: Rutgers University, 1974.

Voorthuizen, E. 'Thatching in Botswana', *Botswana Notes and Records*, vol. 8, Gaborone: The Botswana Society, 1976, p. 169.

Walton, J. *Father of Kindness and Father of Horses*. Lesotho: Morija Printing Works, no date.

————. *African Village*. Pretoria: J.L. van Schaik, 1956.

————. 'South African Peasant Architecture', *African Studies*, 10, 1951, pp. 70—9.

West, M., and Morris, J. *Abantu*. Cape Town: C. Struik, 1976.

Wood, J.G. *The Natural History of Man, Africa*. London: George Routledge and Sons, 1874.

Wrinch-Schulz-Joyce. *Zulu*. South Africa: Purnell, 1975.

Yoffe, M. 'Botswana Basketry', *African Arts*, vol. 12, no. 1, November 1978, pp. 42—7.